CRISIS COUNSELING:
HOPE AND HEALING FOR LIFE'S TRANSITIONS

BY
DR. STAN DEKOVEN

Vision Publishing · Ramona, California

CRISIS COUNSELING

© COPYRIGHT 1995 BY VISION PUBLISHING

2ND EDITION © COPYRIGHT 2004

ISBN: 1-931178-84-4

VISION PUBLISHING
1520 MAIN STREET, SUITE C
RAMONA, CA 92065
760-789-4700
WWW.VISION.EDU/PUBLISHING

PRINTED IN THE UNITED STATES OF AMERICA

Table of Contents

Forward to the Second Edition

Having had the privilege of public and private ministry for some 25 years now, I have observed many crises. Many pastors' families have collapsed in front of me, as they faced and walked through loss and personal tragedy. I have alway considered it a true honor to be called upon in times of need to help God's servants and families.

September 11, 2001, threw the U.S. and much of the world into crisis. The shock soon passed, and a flood of emotions, hurt and fear, anger and sadness, ensued. The response to this crisis is ongoing, the final results to be determined.

I initially wrote this book out of need. We (Vision International College & University) needed a textbook for a course in Crisis Ministry. However, due to my personal crisis (the loss of my spouse of 26 years, Karen), it has become more of a personal journey to help in crisis management and resolution, and assist in grief recovery (see my companion book, *Grief Relief*). It is my sincere hope that for men and women in trouble, and for those tasked to minister to men and women in crisis, that this updated and expanded work will facilitate growth and healing by God's grace.

Stan DeKoven, Ph. D.
President – Vision International College & University

Introduction

"The Lord God said, 'It is not good for the man to be alone. I will make a helper suitable for him...Therefore shall a man leave...and shall cleave unto his wife: and they shall be one flesh'" (Genesis 2:18, 24 KJV).

The Broken Circle

I was twenty-one years old when my beautiful bride and I took that long walk down the aisle of the church. We were both so very excited to finally make official what we were completely sure of. We were made for each other, forever! I still get heart palpitations of joy when I look back at that marvelous event.

One of the most touching parts of our ceremony was the exchanging of our rings. The minister, my good friend and colleague, Dr. Joseph Bohac, recited to us the symbolic significance of this act. The ring symbolized our never-ending love and devotion to each other, the circle of love which was never to be broken. Never!

Well, that's the way it was meant to be. For Karen and me, though we have had our crisis times in our marriage and family, we've survived happily.[1] Yet so many of our friends' marriages have not survived. Though many Christian couples state the same vows as we did, for all too many the eternally pledged circle is broken. But why?

In the United States today, approximately 50% of marriages end in divorce (Christian marriages suffer at an even higher rate), thousands of children are abused physically and sexually, wives are battered, children run away, over 6,000 adolescents annually commit suicide, and families disintegrate. The pressures of our world are immense and most difficult to cope with. Even in our churches we are confronted with the *"besetting sins"* (Hebrews 12:1) that destroy the circle that was to be unbroken.

Over the past few years it has been my privilege to work with many families who were at their breaking point. There has been a renewed interest among secular and Christian circles also to recognize and acknowledge the immensity of the family breakdown. As impressive as the statistics of divorce, abuse, and self-destruction may be, there remain mixed views amongst the church of Jesus Christ as to how we should approach the wounded or broken family. It is apparent that something must be done to stem the tide.

Let me illustrate. It was about 3:00 AM when the phone rang. As I rubbed the sleep from my eyes, I listened intently to a story that I have heard only too often. Late the evening before, a rather well-known member of a local church had been arrested. He was being held in custody for alleged sexual abuse against some children in the church. The pastor, a friend of mine, knew all the principle parties very well, and felt caught. He could clearly sense the outrage of the parents of the children who were abused. He was concerned for the children's welfare. He also experienced a sense of outrage against his friend, a man he had ministered to and fellowshipped with, who had committed this horrible sin.

Yet, he also remembered the Christian commitment of Mr. Jones. He must be terribly frightened, and what about Mrs. Jones? What response would she have? Finally, he had so many questions regarding his own response. What would his church think? What would the Lord do? Excellent questions. Difficult answers!

After I processed through my own feelings of shock and anger (Why me, Lord? I really need the sleep!) I began to explore with this very caring and sensitive pastor some of the options that he and the church might exercise. I have since found that the options that we explored together are typical of evangelical churches and have listed them in their most often used fashion. What would you do?

The Ostrich Approach

Bury it and hide. Pretend that it didn't happen. Think of the harm that could come if anyone found out. A former colleague, Mr. Gary Juleen, once told me of a certain pastor's fears of exposing problems in the church. He likened it to the picking up of a rock. When you do so, the bugs start crawling out! Better to keep the rock where it is (and the inherent church problems) than to expose people's problems, for fear of the repercussions. Let's not let anyone know. We don't want to hurt anyone.

Unfortunately, this was the approach that this local church board (who overruled the pastor) used to deal with the problem. The results were devastating for Mr. Jones, the family involved, and for the church as a whole, as we will see later.

The Cancer Approach

Mr. Jones had obviously sinned grievously, guilty until proven innocent. The church board feared that, "If we continue to offer fellowship to him, the results could be devastating." They concluded, "We must cut him off and give total support to the victims only."

This would certainly be a better solution than the first option. This option does eliminate the "problem" in a hurry. In a hurry is right! Usually it is a hasty decision made out of fear. The use of this option offers much needed support for the victim. It is direct and decisive. But what about Mr. Jones? Where is the compassion he needs? Yes, he has sinned. But in spite of the ugliness of this type of sin, God continues to love Mr. Jones, and desires to restore him. Certainly there are legal consequences for his action. Yet, he still requires restoration through the body of Christ.

The Healing Community

Mr. Jones indeed had sinned in a most destructive and despicable fashion. The sexual abuse of children in our society is one of the leading causes of emotional problems in adults today. The church is not exempt from this sin, as we are now becoming aware. Yet, even in the case of this type of sexual crime and sin, there are some basic principles of operation that we must take in order to fulfill our responsibility in Christ. First, we must confront the situation head on. We must know the facts as best we can. Yet, we must do so with an open mind. Second, we must if possible talk with the responsible parties, offering comfort and support, motivated by love. Although Jesus never excused sin or the sinner, He was willing to love and pardon. Each individual needs to be heard and offered clear opportunity for restoration through repentance. Third, keep all communication confidential, and where necessary, squelch rumors and gossip. There is a natural human tendency to want to know all the details. Fourth, offer continued ministry from the church so that continued restoration might occur. This could include ministry in areas of victim assistance (church support for needed counseling, etc.) and prison outreach. Whatever we do, when one of our own is wounded, even if self inflicted, we must be willing and able to bind up their wounds and allow healing to occur. We must not shoot our wounded.

Most of our churches today are ill prepared to handle such emergencies that will inevitably happen within the family, and the family of God. Few churches have trained laity or pastoral staff who can help in times of real crisis. Yet it is precisely there, between the rock and the hard place, that the love of Christ, carefully and judiciously applied, can most fully and completely "heal the broken hearted and set the captive free."

The Family Crucible

Carl A. Whitaker, M.D. and Augustus Y. Napier, Ph.D. wrote an excellent book on troubled families called *The Family Crucible*. They very ably describe the many forces, inter-psychic and societal, that tear away at the fabric of the family. Today, we see thousands of Christian families, members of the body of believers that is the church, torn apart by forces that are often misunderstood. The church has a tremendous opportunity to assist the troubled family and strengthen the Body of Christ if we can learn to recognize the causes and possible cures of family distress.

To ignore the extensive nature of this problem would be as anathema as to ignore that "all have sinned." It is my hope that all Christians might be fully equipped to minister to those in a time of intense need, to those who are in the family crucible.

10

Then the King will say to those on his right, Come you who are blessed by my Father; take your inheritance, the kingdom prepared for you since the creation of the world. For I was hungry and you gave me something to eat, I was thirsty and you gave me something to drink, I was a stranger and you invited me in, I needed clothes and you clothed me, I was sick and you looked after me, I was in prison and you came to visit me. Then the righteous will answer him, "Lord when did we see you hungry and feed you, or thirsty and give you something to drink? When did we see you a stranger and invite you in, or needing clothes and clothe you? When did we see you sick or in prison and go to visit you?" Then the King will reply, "I tell you the truth, whatever you did for one of the least of these brothers of mine, you did for me." (Matthew 25:34-40)

Within the remainder of this book, it is hoped that you will uncover the dynamics within the family, which cause such distress and breakdown, learn how to minister to the family and its individual members, and hopefully how to prevent the need for such a ministry.

To be mature means to face, and not evade, every fresh crisis that comes.

- Fritz Kunkel

The Chinese use two brush strokes to write the word 'crisis'. One brush stroke stands for danger; the other for opportunity. In a crisis, be aware of the danger-but recognize the opportunity.

- Richard M. Nixon

Crisis Defined

What is crisis?

Webster's Definition: "A turning point in anything; decisive or crucial time, stage or event; a time of great danger or trouble, whose outcome decides whether possible bad consequences will follow."

A crisis is an event, whether a "normal" part of our developmental life or "accident," which temporarily changes our world and necessitates an emotional/spiritual adjustment.

Crises are not of themselves good or bad. Their impact is determined by the meaning one gives to the event, and the feelings generated. Let me illustrate by using the story that opened this book. The event that occurred was a spiritual crisis. The pastor's response, which was natural, was one of fear and virtual immobilization. My response was to answer the questions to the best of my ability. The difference in response was related to two factors.

1) The closeness of the event
2) Perception of the meaning of the event

In either case, a crisis definitely makes us stop and evaluate, seek the Lord, and make the necessary adjustments to cope effectively.

Crisis Management & Brief Treatment

Numerous situational variables may precipitate a crisis, including health emergencies, life-threatening illnesses, family problems, crime-related problems (including violent crime victimizations), and community disasters. The Bureau of Justice Statistics of the United States Department of Justice provides national prevalence estimates on violent crime and victimization.

- 959 children are abducted each day of the year (this finding is based on the recent estimates that 350,000 children are abducted each year).
- 357 individuals are victims of forcible rape each day of the year (this finding is based o the Bureau of Justice Statistics [B.J.S.] Annual Criminal Victimization Rates of over 130,000 rapes each year).

The National Center for Health Statistics and the American Hospital Association each provide nationally representative data on certified suicide fatalities, suicide attempts, and emergency room visits.

- Between 685 and 1,645 individuals attempt suicide each day of the year (this finding is based on the Maris & Associates, 1992 estimates that there are between 250,000 and 600,000 suicide attempts each year).
- 254,820 persons visit emergency rooms each day of the year (American Hospital Association, 1992). The majority of men and women visit a hospital emergency room because of a traumatic event or an acute psychiatric or medical crisis (e.g., gunshot wound, rape, car accident, drug overdose, sexually transmitted disease, or serious life-threatening illness).

The National Cancer Institute, the American Cancer Society, Inc., and the Center for Disease Control (C.D.C.) each provide up-to-date reports on annual incidence rates for the various types of cancer and AIDS.

- 3, 205 new cancer cases are diagnosed each day of the year.

- 140 patients with AIDS die each day of the year and in 1994 alone in CDC projects that there will be 43,000-93,000 newly diagnosed AIDS cases.

Personal variables affect the severity and duration of a crisis. These variables include cognitive processes, behavioral coping skills, typical affective processes (i.e., mood), and prior history of psychopathology. One-year prevalence rates for mental and addictive disorders in the United States were recently reported by a group of prominent epidemiologists. The national prevalence rates are based on a five-year N.I.M.H. Epidemiological Catchment Area (ECA) Program at five study sites in different regions of the United States. In addition to one-year prevalence rates, the researchers measured the percentage of the United States population who utilized medical, mental health, and addiction treatment services over the course of one year (Reiger et al., 1993). Their results show that

- 41,488 adults are diagnosed with affective disorders (bipolar, unipolar major depression, dysthymia) each day of the year. A total annual prevalence rate of 15, 143,000 was estimated for affective disorders.
- 54,887 adults are diagnosed with anxiety disorders (phobia, panic disorder, obsessive-compulsive disorders) each day of the year. A total annual prevalence rate of 20,034,000 was estimated for anxiety disorders.
- 41,244 adults are diagnosed with substance abuse disorders each day of the year. A total annual prevalence rate of 15,054,060 was estimated for alcohol and drug-related disorders.

The national prevalence rates of 15 million affective disorders, 20.03 million anxiety disorders, and 15.05 million alcohol and drug related addictions documented above from the ECA studies may well be significantly underestimated. Ronald Kessler and associates in their lifetime and twelve-month prevalence study of fourteen DSM-III-R psychiatric disorders reported that the prevalence of psychiatric disorders is much higher than previously suspected (Kessler, et al., 1994). This comorbidity survey was based on a stratified, multistage area probability sample of 8,098 noninstitutionalized persons, fifteen to fifty-four years of age, from forty-eight states. Close to 50 percent of the respondents indicated that they had suffered from at least one psychiatric disorder during their lifetime, and nearly 30 percent reported having one or more disorders during the twelve-month period directly prior to the

17

study. The most frequently reported disorders during the previous twelve months were depressive disorders, alcohol dependence, social phobia, and simple phobia. With regard to comorbidity, 56 percent of the respondents with a history of at least one psychiatric disorder, reported having two or more disorders. Rural Americans are less likely when compared to their urban counterparts to suffer from three or more disorders during the previous twelve-month period. A surprising finding was that African-Americans reported much lower prevalence rates of affective and substance abuse disorders than White-Americans, despite the fact that the African-Americans respondents had much lower levels of both education and income than White-Americans. Unfortunately, fewer than 40 percent of the respondents with a lifetime disorder had ever received treatment from a mental health professional, and less than 20 percent of those persons reporting a recent disorder had received crisis intervention, psychotherapy, or other clinical treatment during the past twelve months (Kessler, et al., 1994).

In view of the millions of people encountering acute crises as well as psychiatric disorders each year, the need for crisis intervention and brief treatment is vital. As society-at-large begins to recognize the huge number and impact of acute crisis events, an enormous number of social workers, Christian counselors and psychologists will be needed to help people to cope with and resolve social impairments.

Phases of a Crisis

H. Norman Wright, in his excellent book *Crisis Counseling: Helping People in Crisis and Stress* (Here's Life Publications, 1985), outlines the four primary phases of crisis. They are:

1) Impact
2) Withdrawal Confusion
3) Adjustment
4) Reconstruction/Reconciliation

Most of us have experienced a crisis of some proportion during our lifetime forcing us to make a life adjustment. Knowing what a crisis is and how to manage it is of vital importance in ministry to one another in the body of Christ. Let us begin our study by looking in great detail at the four phases of crisis.

"Crisis may occur when an unexpected traumatic external event is effective in disrupting the balance between a person's internal ego adaptation or homeostatic state and the environment...the unexpected nature of the event and the coping resources of the person will determine the dimensions of the crisis experience."

- Burgess & Lazare, 1976

Crisis Counseling in Everyday Lives

The Four Phases of Crisis

I. Impact

Our initial response to given crisis, whether developmental, such as the birth of a new child, a change in career, a new teenager in the family; or situational, such as an accident, loss of a job, separation and divorce, or death, is determined by the impact that the event has upon us and the meaning that we give it. The impact can only be measured by the response that the individual has toward the crisis situation. For some people, the smallest situations can create great anxiety, sadness or depression. Whereas many others, because of a high tolerance for pain or a fairly peace-oriented spirit, are able to flow through many seemingly severe crises without great difficulty. How we respond depends on many factors including:

1. Our genetic predisposition toward stress
2. Our present spiritual walk
3. Our understanding of the things of God (as outlined within the Word of God)
4. Our support systems such as family and friendships (both within and outside of the body of Christ)
5. Our history in regard to the management of crisis situations in our families

Needless to say, the impact of a crisis cannot be fully understood until the crisis occurs. My father used to have a favorite saying, "One man's meat is another man's poison," meaning that what to one person is a crisis to another is not. We must be willing to be loving and gentle with people in crisis, understanding that different people react differently. We should learn love and tolerance for one another, especially in the midst of a crisis event.

II. Withdrawal/Confusion

Normally when a crisis comes it is difficult for us to understand fully why this could have happened to us. I remember as a young man playing baseball at San Diego State University, I was stealing second base (or at least attempting to) when I felt a very sudden and painful "thud" against the side of my head. As I was sliding into second, I was hit in the side of the head by the baseball thrown at about 90 miles an hour by the opposing team's catcher. This was certainly a type of crisis for me. My first thoughts were that of pain and then of fear that I may have been seriously injured. My initial response was to pull away from everyone and quickly grab ahold of my head in pain. I wanted to stay away from anyone that might come close to me. I specifically remember when my coach attempted to give comfort, my response was to tell him, "Leave me alone! I just want to have some time to myself." I lost my sense of orientation after being hit, not sure of what direction I was supposed to go or how I should respond. Shortly thereafter, my head cleared. However, my initial response was to withdraw, as I felt a sense of confusion and loss.

This is not unusual in times of crisis. When someone loses a loved one or a job, or has some other major change occur in their life, there can be times of withdrawal or confusion that can be virtually immobilizing. It is at those times that people need support and loving, gentle encouragement to assist them in working through the crisis.

III. Adjustment

Because a crisis creates a change, and all change is a bit frightening to us, there must come opportunity for adjustment or acceptance of the change. People will adjust to change and crisis at their own pace, and as I like to say, "In their own elegant style." We must allow time for people to make adjustments; although we must also watch for signs of their fixation in a withdrawn and confused state beyond what is helpful and healthy for them.

This adjustment is very smooth for some but rather difficult and jagged for others. Again, our history of dealing with crises in the past, and our personal

24

genetic makeup and personality, will determine how quickly and smoothly we make adjustment to a life crisis.

IV. Reconstruction/Reconciliation
The final phase of crisis is reconstruction or reconciliation. During this time, we attempt to make final sense, and come to a place of peace in regard to the crisis that has occurred. This takes time and each person will make their peace in their own special way. As Christians, we hope that people will come to reconciliation, understanding God's plan and purpose and how his hand has been involved in the midst of tragedy. It is important as believers that we seek this through wise counsel, through inquiry of the Lord in prayer, and through study of the Word of God.

I wish there was a magic cure for all the situations pastors/counselors face in their noble attempt to ease the pain and suffering of crisis. There is not one specific winning strategy. Thus, more important than our clinical skill (though greater skills should be sought) or theological understandings (grow in our knowledge of God and his word we must) is our ministry presence...just, being a loving, vulnerable, listening ear for the one in crisis. Being there in a time of transition can be the most helpful ministry we give.

Then the Lord God called to the man and said to him, "Where are you?" He said, "I heard the sound of You in the garden, and I was afraid because I was naked, so I hid myself," And He said, *"Who told you that you were naked?"*

- Genesis 3:9-11

The Bible and Crisis

If you were to take time to read the Word of God with the specific goal of determining how many crises occurred throughout the Bible, copious amounts of time would be spend outlining such events. The Bible is filled with change, crazy situations, gross immorality, and tremendous miracles presenting the hand of God in the midst of difficult times. In much of the history of the children of Israel, beginning with Adam and Eve's crisis in the garden through the Babylonian exile, we see crisis situations coming, being resolved, adjustment being made, and hopefully, reconciliation occurring for the better. In fact one scholar has said the children of Israel's path throughout history was one of:

1. Walking with God
2. Gross rebellion and rejection of the plans of God
3. Reconciliation and restoration back to God

We also see in the lives and ministries of Christ and the apostles' times of great crisis. These were times that try men's souls where the children of God were at risk yet the power of God moved in great measure.

Briefly outlined here are a few typifying crises, from the Old and the New Testaments, to help us understand what the Word of God says about crises and our response to them.

"The Devil Made Me Do It"

In the beginning, God. From the very beginning God created all things well. But certainly not all things that we experience are good. The reality is we do have troubles as people living in this sin oriented world. The Word of God says that Satan is the god of this world (though defeated) and that sin does abound. Though we can be thankful that grace, as the apostle Paul says, "does even more abound."

From the very beginning of time, when God created something out of nothing, He created his universe in perfect order. When man sinned in the Garden of Eden a devestating change in the way we operate as people began. In Genesis chapter three we see the account of the temptation and deception of Eve, Adam's fall into

29

three we see the account of the temptation and deception of Eve, Adam's fall into sin and their response when God visited them. First of all, it is important to realize that, up until this point, Adam and Eve were perfect (innocent), created whole in the image of God. They had a wonderfully intimate relationship with God. They communed with Him daily. There was no such thing as thorns, or crises of life. They were functional; they had work to do that was meaningful; and they had dominion over all things that God had created. When the fall came things radically changed. Reading in Genesis 3, we begin to see what things changed because of sin. Sin, in and of itself, is a form of crisis.

And the eyes of both of them were opened, and they realized they were naked; so they sewed fig leaves together and made coverings for themselves. Then the man and his wife heard the sound of the Lord God as he was walking in the garden in the cool of the day, and they hid from the Lord God among the trees of the garden. But the Lord God called to the man, "Where are you?" He answered, "I heard you in the garden, and I was afraid because I was naked; so I hid." And he said, "Who told you that you were naked? Have you eaten from the tree that I commanded you not to eat from?" The man said, "The woman you put here with me- she gave me some fruit from the tree, and I ate it." Then the Lord God said to the woman, "What is this you have done." The woman said, "The serpent deceived me, and I ate." (Genesis 3:7-13)

As you continue through the chapter you see the consequences that came upon mankind because of their sin, but also the great promise of God that one would be sent who would bruise the head of the serpent, one who would ultimately defeat Satan and create for us the opportunity of eternal life through Jesus Christ.

There are some interesting points to make in regard to the crisis caused by sin, resulting in our separation from God. First of all, their eyes were opened (vs. 7), they saw things from an entirely different viewpoint than they had before. Prior to their fall they saw things from God's perfect perspective. Their perception of life was without distortion. But, because of the fall they could

30

see not only their own nakedness, but their vulnerability. They began to see things from a natural, rather than a godly viewpoint. The reality is, if we were not human beings we would not experience the pain of crisis. However, we are human, and therefore suffer the consequences of being human. Part of that consequence is that we cannot fully perceive life from God's perspective as intended. Instead we have a distorted worldview. Because of that distorted view, when a crisis comes, regardless of the source of the crisis, whether self-induced or caused by the circumstances of life, we rarely respond according to God's perfect plan.

It is also interesting that Adam and Eve immediately attempted to hide themselves because they recognized their nakedness. Because of their vulnerability they attempted to withdraw and to cover themselves from their shame. For many of the crises that we will look at throughout the rest of this book, an experience of guilt and shame often accompany the crisis. Some of this is to be expected if personal sin has brought us to crisis. But ultimately we must recognize that attempting to hide and withdraw will not resolve the crisis, but in many cases will only worsen it. God wants us to seek the answer to every problem in life through a deeper relationship with Jesus Christ, and to clearly understand His plan and purpose found in His Word.

You will further note that when confronted with the statement, *"Who told you that you were naked?"* Adam responded, *"The woman you put here with me - she gave me some fruit from the tree, and I ate it."* We call that a projection. Adam projected the blame and the responsibility for his choice onto another. You will find that many people will do this while in the middle of a crisis. "So and so made me do it!" "It's because of my mother!" "It's because of this or that problem within my life!" One of the first steps toward growth in any situation is the owning of responsibility. In spite of what has happened or what the situation is, I am responsible to do something with it now. Again, this does not refer to those that were victimized children through child abuse. Other than children, no matter what happens, we are responsible for how we respond. Perhaps we are not responsible for the crisis itself, but we must own responsibility for our response if intervention, healing and relief are to come.

31

Adam's and Eve's response is typical of the natural or human response to crises. Let's look at God's response. It is common for a parent who becomes upset with his/her child to respond with anger and "send them to their room". However, the Lord's response was different, even unexpected. In the midst of their rebellion and disobedience God comes to them, asking leading questions to provide opportunity for repentance leading to restoration and healing. Of course, they refused his garland.

Immediately, God looked after the protection of His children and gave a promise. In spite of the consequences of our sin, He would make a provision for us, showing us the way to right standing with God. One of the beauties of the Old Testament, whether we look at the story of Jacob and Esau, Joseph, Gideon, Samson, Nehemiah, or Esther, we see God, in spite of wrong decisions, bad situations, and terrible circumstances providing a way of escape in time of need. In spite of the rebellion, the disenchantment and the stubbornness of the children of Israel over the years, God would always find a way to assist them through their crises. We know that He is continuing to do that for us, even today.

"Help! I'm Sinking"

Let's look at another crisis. This one from the New Testament. In Matthew chapter fourteen we see the story of Peter walking on the water. Many of us are very familiar with this Bible story. Jesus walked out on the water toward His disciples who were already on the Sea of Galilee.

"When the disciples saw Him walking on the lake, they were terrified. *'It's a ghost,'* they said, and cried out in fear. But Jesus immediately said to them: ' *Take courage! It is I. don't be afraid.' 'Lord, if it's you, 'Peter replied, 'tell me to come to you on the water"* (Matthew 14:26-28).

As we know, Peter was bid by Jesus to come. Peter, jumping out of the boat, began to walk on the water toward Jesus. Many in the church world criticize Peter for not having enough faith to walk all the way out to Jesus, having a

32

wonderful stroll on top of the waves that were being tossed to and fro. We should not forget, however, that he did walk on the water!

Peter began to take his eyes off Christ because of his fear, he began to sink. Just prior to sinking, he recognized that the storm about him was too powerful for him to survive. He cried out to the Lord saying, "*Lord save me!*" The Word of God says that Jesus was there to rescue Peter from his difficult crisis situation, taking him back into the boat, removing him from danger. From that experience all the disciples recognized Jesus as the Messiah, and worshipped Him.

Again, there are some interesting points to make from this crisis situation.

First of all, Peter, in an act of faith, wanted to be with Jesus. Yet, in spite of his faith he stepped out into a situation that was clearly over his head. Many of the crises of life, if you will, are self-induced. They are not always caused by bad luck or bad breaks. Such was the case with Peter. He stepped out with every good intention and yet became swallowed up in the affairs of life. He recognized that he was in a situation that was so far above his ability to cope, so he began to sink, most likely in great despair. How many of us would have felt the same as Peter did, without hope? And yet, Peter, being as bright as he was, did the one thing that would save him. He cried out to the Lord for help.

As one ministers in counseling to people in crisis, one of the first steps toward resolving a crisis situation is recognizing one's inability to fully cope with the situation on their own. Peter recognized that he was out of his element. He would not be able to survive the situation, so he cried out to the Lord Jesus who was immediately there for him. One of our responsibilities as counselors is to help people to understand that they have hope in Christ. In the midst of their difficulties, Jesus will be there for them. Perhaps not always as immediately as in this situation, but we know that God will see them through any predicament.

There are so many other New Testament stories, from Paul's crisis in Ephesus, to Stephen's stoning, to Peter's time in prison, where God miraculously delivered in the time of crisis. We, as believers, must recognize that Jesus does have the power to deliver us. We must also recognize that living life has its risks and problems. There is no guarantee that there will be a bridge over troubled waters, but only a way through the troubled waters we must traverse.

Probably our best example of one who understood what it meant to be in a time of trouble was King David of Israel. Many of his Songs are songs crying out to God for protection against the enemies that were chasing him. Many of his psalms speak of the anguish that he experienced and the fear that he would be swallowed up in the trials of life. We also rejoice with David as we see how God delivered him from his many trials.

At the end of this book you will find some Scriptures that are designed to assist people, to comfort them in times of trouble. Many are from David's psalms and from Solomon's proverbs. Let it be known that God understands that we are frail and fragile people and yet, in spite of the difficulties we face, there is no question that God shall supply all of our needs according to His riches in glory by Christ Jesus (Philippians 4:19) Notice it is not according to our needs, but according to His riches that He supplies. Further, Proverbs 3:5-6, probably the strongest Scripture to indicate God's ability to see us through, says *"Trust in the Lord with all your heart and lean not on your own understanding; in all your ways acknowledge him, and he will make your paths straight."*

It is important that as people go through the crises of life they understand that the Word of God is a comfort and guide. It will assist us; it will help us and direct us to a place of fulfillment in Him. It takes time, grace, and God's mercy to go through critical life changes. We will now look at various developmental crises, or *"stage"* crises, and God's answers for them.

**Close scrutiny will show that most "crisis situations"
are opportunities to either advance, or stay where you
are.**
- Dr. Maxwell Maltz

SECTION ONE

Developmental Crises

Times of Transition
A developmental crisis can best be defined as one that occurs during the normal transition times of life. Those primary transition times that are presented within this book include:

1) Marriage
2) Childbirth
3) Child rearing
4) Career changes and development
5) Mid-life transitions
6) Teenagers
7) Empty nest
8) Senior years

There are many situations that can occur which are not necessarily crises, but times of change, which must be adapted to. Let's look first at the crisis, or transition, that we call marriage, through the story of the Johnson's, a true tale though altered to provide anonimity. Their story will illustrate the potential pressures that can bear down on a marriage, possibly leading to crisis. Perhaps you will see yourself or someone you minister to through their story.

George and Wendy Johnson were a wonderful couple. When they first met, they were filled with a romantic/innocent desire to have the perfect marriage. Both were believers, George had been a committed Christian since a young boy, having met Christ through the Sunday School at his church. Though he had waned some in fervor, he had a fairly strong knowledge of the word of God and desire to live right according to scripture. In fact, both his mom and dad were believers, dad was a deacon at the church, and they had a fairly traditional family life with minimal upheaval during George's formative years.

Wendy "got saved" during a crisis time in her early adolescence. In her freshman year it was discovered that her father had had an affair, leading to a very nasty divorce. A girl friend had led her to Christ at a special youth rally. She has been faithful to God, though battled some with her faith.

The Johnson's married after about 18 months of courtship (both had just turned 22), and all would have predicted success in spite their relatively young start.

Seeds of faith are always within us; sometimes it takes a crisis to nourish and encourage their growth.

- Susan Taylor

Chapter 1

Marriage

From our earliest days, most of us, especially within western culture, look forward to the time when we will find that perfect mate, our spouse. The Word of God says that he who has found a wife has found a good thing. We also know from the Bible that it was God's original intention (as seen in Genesis 2) that a man and a woman should find each other, leave their families of origin, and unite together in what should be the greatest adventure and the most intimate relationship that two human beings can ever experience. We call that marriage.

For those of us who are married[2], we recognize that the ideal or perfect relationship that meets all of our deepest longings and needs, is more a fabrication of a romanticized society than a reality of our actual experience. Let me not be morose about this. Certainly, marriage can be and should be a most exciting and wonderful experience. For most of us I hope it has been. Yet, in the midst of all the romance and the excitement of a relationship, a marriage takes hard work and dedication to make it successful.

Let's first look at some of the dynamics that make up a healthy relationship. Then we will look at some of the crisis issues that can tear down the fabric of this wonderful relationship that is a type of Christ's relationship with the church. The first dynamic we will address is the **family of origin**. As I say in many seminars, "If I had never had parents, I'd never be crazy!" What I mean by that is, I have learned how to behave, what to expect, how to respond in certain situations, especially crises, within the context of my family of origin. The experiences, the treatment, the relationship that I had with my mother and father has strongly shaped many of my perceptions of the way I am supposed to be as a husband and father and how my wife is to be as a woman in relationship with me and our children.

41

It is fairly easy to see how problematic this could be in real experience. Let me give you an example. When I was first married, being raised in a family that was very expressive emotionally, my assumption was that if there were problems within a relationship, you would yell and scream and argue it out over a 5 to 10 minute period, call each other names and 15 minutes later, take each other to lunch. That was the way things were handled in my family. Individual's boundaries were constantly violated. In my wife's family, however, they were relatively silent in their expression of feelings and emotions. They were unable to share feelings on an intimate level. They very rarely argued. If there was a conflict they would withdraw and allow it to pass with time. Nothing was ever fully resolved. You can see how this difference in style would be problematic for my wife and me in our earliest relationship. When I would want to have a good fight and get it over with I'd yell and express my feelings and then wonder why 15-20 minutes later she was still emotionally bleeding all over the place, unable to talk or respond to me. That would create great frustration in me. I felt rejected by her and she felt attacked by me.

This is typical of many relationships. They start out with the greatest of intentions but because of an unawareness of differences in style, an atmosphere where crisis can occur is created.

The marriage dyad, that is the relationship between the two adults, is the most important part of family life. Conflict within a relationship can be linked, many times, to the family of origin and unresolved conflicts between the spouse and the family they were raised in.

Most difficulties within a relationship can be seen as tension that is unresolved between the two because of poor communication or lack of understanding of one another. In reality, in families there are several roles that can be taken which can be dysfunctional or can cause problems. They include the roles of:

1) Placator, who is a person who attempts to smooth things out no matter what the cost
2) Blamer, one who attacks the other in hope of becoming the topdog versus the underdog

3) Irrelevant one, one who constantly tries to change the subject or throw temper tantrums in order to throw things off the track
4) Super reasonable one, that is always trying to stay cool, calm, and collected while the other looks like an orangutan out of control

All of these are roles that can be played, however they are highly dysfunctional and create problems for the future. God intended our marriages to be happy and successful, and to be a model to the body of Christ, demonstrating the strength of God to create a binding relationship that will last forever. God's plan and ideal is one man, one woman, one lifetime, not divorce, remarriage and all that goes with that. At the same time we must be clear that these crises can occur, just because one gets married, as each party brings their past into their present.

What are some of the possible crises in marriage? What are some of the milestones that you can look forward to in a marriage relationship?

The One Year Wonder

For Wendy and George, their first year was rocky at best. George was a very serious guy who lived in a matriarchal family system. Mom had all the power, and mom did everything for everyone (whether wanted or not). Wendy came, in spite of the divorce, from an egalitarian family. Further, most likely due to the divorce and dads treachery, she had certain insecurities and wanted constant reassurance of George's love and fidelity. To their benefit, they remained close to the youth pastor and his wife who helped them pray through their many small but potentially damaging hurts. They had a rough go, but with good support, lots of honest prayer and a willingness to change, they made it through year one with relationship in tact.

The first year of marriage is by far the most difficult in regard to adjustment. As mentioned above, a couple will enter a relationship starry-eyed, deaf, dumb, (and often stupid). They have great hopes that every deficiency within their life, that they have brought into the relationship, will be healed and resolved because of the "*love*" of the spouse.

43

The reality is that two half people do not make a whole. They only make two half people trying to struggle together to become whole. It takes two whole people to make each other whole and not one of us fit the bill completely. That is why we have a need to have that wonderful, spiritual relationship with the Lord Jesus Christ and to be able to share that with one another. The first year of marriage can be quite critical. In fact the highest incidence of divorce occurs within the first year of marriage.

Because of this, pre-marital counseling is strongly recommended to ensure that problems are resolved before the big plunge. Further, churches should be aware of the special tensions of adjustment that occur during this first year.

The Seven Year Itch

By the seventh year, George had been promoted to a management position, requiring long days and occasional weekends. Two children had arrived, ages 4 and 2, and the responsibilities of house, job, church etc. were piling up. As often occurs, parallel lives for Wendy and George had emerged. George was working 10 hour days and occasional weekends to "properly provide" for his growing family, coming home tired, finding an equally exhausted Wendy. Worn to a frazzle by her home responsibilities, she took a part-time job (even though her check went mostly to daycare) in order to cope with being cooped up with the kids all day.

Tensions mounted, requiring they seek some help; to manage their burgeoning loneliness and occasional outburst of stress on each other.

The counseling, brief but effective, focused upon a re-evaluation of their core values, a re-affirmation of their covenant with each other, and a new determination to make adjustments to meet each other's needs. Simply talking about the problems helped (after the initial blame game towards each other) and real crisis was adverted. So it can be with any/all developmental crisis. De-escalation through clear and direct communication can frequently lead to

44

new levels of commitment and intimacy...assuming problems have not become to great, secretive or bitter.

Second to the potential problems of the first year of marriage is what we call the "seven year itch." This corresponds to the settling in period of the reality of the responsibilities of child rearing, career, and future. It is about this time that couples turn over in bed, look at each other and wonder, "Who is this person that I'm sleeping with?" The time has come to re-evaluate what is important in their life. What do they want to do? Is this the person they want to spend their life with? The Lord would want us to take the time to re-evaluate, to see the need for a continuing relationship, not to bail out, run and choose the easy way of divorce to get out of a situation that makes us feel uncomfortable.

Other Transitions

After that come the fifteen-year, twenty-five-year, and forty-year marks which are also times of transition. These times of transition provide opportunities to evaluate what is most important in life. It is an opportunity to recommit ourselves to our relationship with our spouse.

Specific crises can occur, both situational and within the developmental stages, as we visit parenting, adolescents, mid-life, latter years, divorce, death, etc. Let it suffice to say in this section that marriage is the foundation upon which family life is built. That marriage foundation must be constantly strengthened and renewed through good communication, clear role expectations, a great deal of love and forgiveness, and through a heavy dosage of spiritual strength from the Lord. Those marriages where partners have committed themselves to walk with God, to pray, to fellowship with positive members of the body of Christ, and have made a clear decision in their mind that they will, under no circumstances violate the commitment they have made to one another, will not only survive the stresses of marriage but will thrive. They grow to become like those beautiful, old couples who walk the road hand in hand with a twinkle in their eyes. You see the twinkle and you know that there is something very special only they share with one another. It is the end result of two people who are committed to one another through thick and thin.

Chapter 2

Childbirth and Parenting

Although we would not call the birth of a child a crisis, it is still a major cause of stress in many relationships.

The Word of God declares that children are a blessing from the Lord. A blessing requiring commitment and courage. I have heard it said, "Oh! I wish we could go back to the good old days." Why? The truth is "childhood is a time of undiluted pleasure is like a fiction story, concocted by adults who have chosen to forget the melancholy anguish that accompanies childhood." (Sadly, reference lost).

For the average parent pain, fear and worry as to what is going on and whether or not their child's needs will be met caress the days and nights of childhood. Events and experiences in their young lives may leave deep scars and hurts. Not only is the child's physical life a concern, but his or her psychological and emotional well-being can be affected. Angry shouts of parents, as well as long periods of tension-filled silence can result in damaging a child's emotional welfare. An uncaring remark by a teacher or friend can have an effect on his/her self-esteem and how he/she feels about themselves.

Family problems can disrupt a comfortable parent/child relationship. Frequent moves, unemployment, financial hardship, illness, death of a friend or family member, or divorce can dramatically change a happy home into a stressful living situation. The family is both a source of protection and a target of attack. The child's sense of value, including his/her self worth, is substantially influenced by what he/she experiences in the family. Anxious, uncomfortable parents cause the children to experience what they perceive to be instability and he or she becomes fearful and loses trust in self and in others. Affection, safety, nurture, and stability are such simple needs. But, if these needs are not met within the first few years of life, scars will remain and the needs may never be met fully.

Childbirth and child rearing is a major transition for most of us. It is not something to be taken lightly, but should be planned well and considered fully. This major transition changes the overall focus of our life pattern as parents. It requires two individuals who are willing to mature to the extent that they can subordinate their personal needs to those of a child. I remember so well when my wife and I had our first child. We had such a desire to raise that perfect little girl. We wanted her to emulate all the good and wonderful things found within the Word of God. What we found was that she was not always fully cooperative in becoming what we wanted her to be. Our child, and now both of our children, have had their ups and downs. They were demanding at times. Their birth required a profound adjustment on our part to raise them in any form of successful manner.

Some of the crises that can occur within a family when a child is introduced into the home are as follows:

Focus of Attention

First of all, the wife instinctively focuses her life's attention on the needs of the child. This is natural but at the same time can be taken to an extreme. As previously mentioned, the primary relationship of the family is that of the marriage. Wives who have not had a positive communicative relationship with their husbands can focus so much of their time and attention on the child they neglect the ligitimate needs of their husband.

Fathers in turn may feel neglected and left out. For a period of time they have been the number one person in their wife's life. This is reminiscent on a rather unconscious level of how important they were when they were a child with their mother. It feels wonderful to have that special attachment. In many ways, when a child comes into the home, that attachment must change. The mother must focus on the needs of the child more than on those of the husband. Jealousy can enter in, as well as arguments, bitterness, and rivalries of all sorts.

This may sound quite silly to many but it happens all too often. I remember one family I was counseling, the husband was so insanely jealous, and so angry that the wife's attentions had been turned toward the needs of her son, that he determined, at that point in his life, never to suffer that kind of "rejection" or "abandonment" ever again. He determined in his mind that when this child became mature enough he would divorce his wife and move on with his life. This was in spite of what the Word of God says or the counsel he received. What a terrible decision and one that destroyed a potentially wonderful family because of hurt, anguish, and an inability to adjust.

Bringing a child into the home with 2:00 a.m. feedings, crying fits, need for attention, etc. can lead to conflict between a husband and wife. If resentment builds and there is not adequate communication and a spirit of tolerance and forgiveness in the home, it can lead to bitterness and even emotional, psychological separation. This happens too often and sets the stage for a very difficult empty nest crisis, which we will look at later in this book.

It is important that we keep much of our cultural and societal changes in the proper perspective. If you remember back in the 1950's in the United States, you are aware of many changes, especially in regard to birth control, which altered the way in which families develop. Up to that time, when people married, they had children. That was normal. Now, parents tend to wait a period of time before children come into the home. In the mid-60's there was a sharp increase in the divorce rate which coincide with the employment of women outside of the home. This has continued into the present, which has caused necessary restructuring of the family role. There are many things that must be talked through in regard to mothering and fathering which were not important in years past. They include the demands of child care, issues relating to roles, such as cleaning and maintaining homes and working with children, scheduling of time with one another, the two-income family, all of these require the ability to be flexible and considerate in dealing with the problems and crises that can occur when a child comes into the home.

Furthermore, couples must be able to come into agreement in regards to the style of discipline, ways of communicating and with the general care for a

49

child. Most of us have a model of parenting in our minds, which we learned in the fertile soil of our family of origin. Not that our families of origin were necessarily better or more functional than our spouse's, but because it is more comfortable, we tend to repeat similar patterns. If we were abused or neglected, we might become aggressive or abusive, or a victim ourselves. If our parents spanked, we will tend to spank. If they used time out, we likely will use time out. If they were over-indulgent, we would tend to be over-indulgent. Or we might flip to the other end of the spectrum in rebellion to the way our parents raised us. That is why it is so important for parents to refer to the Word of God and to wise counsel, preferably before they have children, to ascertain what a Biblical model of discipline in, and the behavior that parents can both agree to and operate in. Nobody's parents were perfect; therefore, we're not going to be perfect parents. That is a myth within American society: the myth of perfection. We need to recognize that all we can do is the very best we can. We must learn to love and discipline our children according to Biblical standards, for their benefit, not the parents.

Another point to remember is that as parents we often have high expectations as to the gender and also the personality and gifts of the child we are going to have. Most parents carry high hopes as to how their child is going to live their life, and what they are going to be in the future. If we press too strongly our wants and wishes upon our children, we can hurt them in their overall psychological development. This can be seen in family systems that are highly dysfunctional. An example of this would be if a father, who tends to be a very aggressive and domineering person, has a son who tends to be more passive and easy going. If the father believes that the only way to be successful is to be hard driving, and attempts to force his child into that mold, the child will learn, in an attempt to please the parent, to pretend to be what Dad wants him to be. This is the beginning of the development of a false self that so many carry within the world and the church.

In the movement of the Adult Children of Alcoholics and Adults Raised in Dysfunctional Families we see that poor communication, neglect, and unobtainable parental expectations are some of the primary, underlying causes of psychological symptoms such as depressions, fears, etc. They have learned that they cannot be who they are, as created by God, but they must become something else to be accepted and affirmed. This role, or false self, becomes so pervasive that they rarely know that it is not really them at all. One of the things that Christ does, when He comes into our lives by His Holy Spirit, is to communicate to us through the written word who we really are. Ultimate significance is gained through acknowledging our uniqueness from God's perspective. He has the power to heal most damaged areas of our lives. As parents it is important that we recognize the needs of our children and have the maturity to reach out to meet their needs, not just to meet our own.

Conflict within families is inevitable. It is important to recognize that there are two primary needs that all of us require.

To have a sense of:
1. Security and safety
2. Acceptance and love

Security, safety, love, or acceptance are primary needs that all people have, and God intends that we have those needs met. It is not the need that is really a problem, but it is the strategies that we utilize to meet the need. If we, as parents, can create a happy healthy family environment, we can significantly minimize the problems that our children have within the family relationship.

There are some simple examples of discipline styles that are effective for children, and along with certain guidelines that can be used in dealing with our children. They can be found in my book, *Parenting on Purpose.* I would encourage you to read and study this book in detail. Let it be known that if, as parents, we do not adequately care for our children, they will not get better with time. Things will usually get worse.

Chapter 3

Teenagers

The teenage years are not truly a crisis, although many critical themes are acted out within the high school years. Adolescence is not a disease as many parents seem to think. However, it is a time, of many changes. Many difficult struggles can occur within teenage years. Adolscence is a time when a boy or girl is beginning to emerge into a young man or woman. There are significant biological changes, sociological changes, emotional and intellectual changes that are occurring during the adolescent period.

In this section we will look at some of the primary crisis situations that can occur during the adolescent period, and hopefully assist you in preparing yourself for these possible crises, whether you are in the role of parent or in the role of minister/counselor.

Depression

Depression[3] is a too common problem for adolescents that can lead to crisis. What is depression and how does it develop? Depression is defined as a chronic disturbance of mood that involves a profound sense of sadness, lack of energy, and irritability, both in children and adults. The irritability can especially be found in children. This happens more times than not and can have up to one year in duration, but it is not what we call the occasional blues. Most adolescents, as those of you who have experienced an adolescent in your home know, can be very, very moody. We are not talking about the normal "moodiness" of the up and down you see in a typical adolescent. This is a long-term form of mood that is profoundly sad, with a lack of energy, etc. Some of the symptoms include poor appetite or overeating, insomnia or hypersomnolence, low energy or fatigue, low self-esteem, poor concentration, difficulty in making decisions, and feelings of despair or hopelessness. As we survey this list, most of us can identify, at one time or another, with each of these symptoms. The difference between us and those that have actual depression is that these symptoms are pervasive, of a long term nature, not just a periodic feeling, attitude, or belief system.

What are the causes of depression? There are many. We will name just a few.

1. Genetic and/or Physical: Improper diet, lack of exercise, poor rest, low blood sugar, and abuse of alcohol or drugs can cause some of these conditions. Further there seems to be a genetic predisposition toward depression. My personal belief is that even in those cases, God, by His Spirit through the ministry of the laying on of hands and prayer, can break those predisposed conditions in our lives. Someone who has a history of long-term depression linked to their mother's or father's depression can be freed instantaneously by the power of God. For most, longer term care is needed. Even after that, however, there is a need for discipleship, learning, and growth to be able to live a life without recurring symptoms.

2. The Family Systems View: In some families where adolescents become depressed there seems to have been a lack of warmth, rejection and abandonment, or trauma that has occurred in childhood. Most of us have been raised in families that were quite imperfect. When we think back upon our families, if we were not accepted for the way we were, we tended towards a false sense of self that we thought to be our true identity. When we recognize that we have lived a form of lie in order to survive, the results can be depression. Yet, if we really understand who we are in Christ, we recognize that in spite of what has occurred in our past we are able, within the body of Christ, through prayer, counsel, and the reading and understanding of God's Word, to overcome the most traumatic of childhoods.

3. Learned Helplessness: This is a victim syndrome whereby someone who has been significantly victimized through life will learn to respond in a helpless and hopeless fashion. They develop a sense of inadequacy, which is quite pervasive. This too can be overcome and we will see

some of the ways we can do so in the section on counseling techniques for crisis.

4. Negative Thinking: The Word of God, when it is talking about the negative side of our old nature in Proverbs, says, "As a man thinks in his heart, so is he." Renowned psychiatrist, Aaron Beck, has said that our thinking causes our emotions, not vice versa. We used to think that if you feel bad, you will think bad, or if you behave wrongly, you will think and feel bad. The science of human behavior has again confirmed the Word of God in that it is the thinking process that is most important. If you think badly of self and of the world, if you are critical and condemning, you will tend to be blue or depressed most of the time.

There are other areas that are worth noting, including life stresses, anger that is turned against the self (especially when we have been hurt and seek revenge), guilt over past sins or problems, and loss.

What are the effects of depression? They can be many including, psychosomatic illness, poor performance, unhappiness, masked reactions such as drug involvement, impulsive behavior, including sexual acting out, withdrawal, and ultimately suicide.

Briefly, how do we treat depression? Normally through a combination of talk therapy or counseling, and in some cases, medication. The primary course of care is to encourage the individual to talk about the circumstances they are facing and to assist them to change the way they think about their situation. It is important that people express their feelings but not wallow in them. The prodigal son is a good example of one who was depressed, mostly because of his own choices. He did end up, without question, in a pigpen. He wallowed in it, but only long enough to come to himself, at which point he changed the focus of his thinking. He needed to get up, get cleaned up, and go back to his father's house. So it is with people that you will counsel. It is important that, although you allow them to talk about their feelings, they don't dwell on them, ad nauseam. Help them through the Word of God, prayer, and through direct confrontation to begin to see themselves through God's eyes, not through the eyes of the situation.

Secondly, it helps to change the environment. Sometimes a change of routine, starting to walk, writing out feelings, seeking forgiveness, forgiving others, getting involved with other projects and people can be very important in overcoming depression.

Finally, teach them to find a purpose for living, a meaning beyond themselves. As Christians that should be easy as we have life in God and a purpose in Him; that is to praise God and to serve others for the Lord Jesus Christ.

Another major area of crisis is that of teen suicide. Suicide, which can be the ultimate response to depression in a child, has been on the rise within western culture in astronomical proportions within the last few years. The topic of suicide is covered more fully in the "Situational Crisis" section of this book.[3]

Career[4] Development and the Crisis of the Loss of a Job

A few years ago, I was asked to address a group of men who had been unemployed for a period in excess of six months. When I came to speak to this group, I was amazed at how devastating was the loss of their career, and their feeling of despair. Many had a belief that their career options had ended. Especially in the United States, and primarily for men, although women experience this to an extent, one's career, or one's job or ability to earn a living is a major source of identity and self-esteem. When women gather to talk with each other about their lives, most will talk about their home, their children, and their husbands. Men will primarily ask of each other, after learning each others names, "What do you do for a living?" So much of a man's identity is linked to his career.

The thought of a career and what we are going to do with our lives begins in our early childhood. We tend to take on certain roles, and play games as children to try to determine, "What are we going to be when we grow up?" Very few of us grow up to fulfill our childhood fantasies. Life circumstances

56

and opportunities may shade outcomes. Work and career goals are important in our self-esteem development and in our overall life script, or plan.

An illustration of this and of the importance and power of those childhood fantasies can be seen in my personal life. When I was a young man, my primary ambition in life was to play professional baseball. All through elementary school, high school, and even through college, I played baseball with a modicum of success. I had a great ambition to continue on into the pro ranks, but I had one small problem; I had a call of God upon my life. In time I had to make a major decision. Was I going to pursue the ministry, especially in the area of counseling hurting people, or was I going to continue on toward my childhood dream. The decision was not difficult, after it was made. I had a much higher calling than to give it my best shot at professional baseball. I moved on into ministry. As I look back, however, I see that it was a monumental decision. The greatest difficulty for me was I still carried a fantasy about being a great star and having all the world beating a path to my door. In reality, even as the apostle Paul said, I had to put away childish things in order to move into the career and life goals that God had for me, and that were pleasing to the Lord.

The decision for a career is a tremendous one. The decision made is not always based upon logic, but often upon history or influences of other types. Some, because they wish to please their father or mother, choose a career in line with what the parents feel is best for them. In some cases, the young adult will choose a career in rebellion against the parent for the same reasons. In choosing a career, it is best to seek the will of God through wise counsel from trusted leaders in the body of Christ.

The career choice made in our late teens and early twenties is important for the development of our self-esteem in the future. Generally speaking, the career choices that we make in our teens do not last through the rest of our lives. Research has shown that adult identity is not solidified until approximately age thirty. It is interesting to note that Jesus began His public ministry at approximately that age, lining up with the tradition of the priesthood. Secondly, for many young men and women, the first major re-evaluation of, "Who am I? What do

I want to do with my life?" occurs at around age thirty. Many major career decisions and changes are made during this natural time of transition.

Career choices, which are a natural part of our emotional, physical, and financial development, need to be made with our eyes wide open. It is helpful to gather considerable information about what you can do, and would like to do, with your life. It would be wise to take certain standardized vocational inventories, which are administered by high school and college career counselors. These give the individual an idea of what his desires are, and ultimately what he/she would be successful at. The Word of God says that if we delight ourselves in the Lord, He will give us the desires of our heart (Psalms 37:4). Many people delight themselves in the Lord through praise, worship, and seeking after God, but since they do not fully understand the desires of their own heart, they do not know what it is they need to will unto the Father. They do not know how to walk in His perfect and most holy will because they are unable to discern what they really want to do with their lives. A major problem with many in the body of Christ is an inability to will, to determine, or to make a decision. It is important, as early as possible within the teenage years, to determine what career options one has, according to their behavioral style.

Secondly, it is important to seek the heart of God. It is also important to seek wise counsel. Chat with others who have career experience in the same area of your interest. Find out what the requirements are. Is it worth the cost for the individual student or worker to pay in order to be in a certain career field? It is also important to think of the future. What are the possibilities for longevity in the field that you are choosing? Many who chose to work in unskilled labor fields are finding themselves, because of a lack of education, unable to adequately provide for their family. This is tragic. However, for most of us, this tragedy can be avoided.

Finally, it is important to recognize that a career is just one part of an individual's life responsibilities. It is good to have goals, dreams and visions about what you would like to do when you grow older, but it is most important that we seek first the kingdom of God and His righteousness, and all things we need will be added unto us (Matt 6:33). It is important that we subordinate our career goals to the overall goal of following Christ with all of our hearts.

Loss of Job

The loss of a job can be devastating. I still remember the first time that I quit a job under duress. I had been working in a Christian ministry, which had promised me advancement, but their promises were not based in reality. At the time, my wife was pregnant. We had very few options to speak of that we could see, other than that we needed to leave the job we were in. The job included housing and a salary, both of which were disappearing due to our necessary but difficult decision. I made the decision to leave that job, hoping that I would be able to find another one quickly, but unfortunately I was unable to. Further, I was in the midst of completing a Masters degree in counseling, but had run out of money to accomplish that task. So with very few options left to me, we moved in with our in-laws, who were very gracious to take us in under trying circumstances. The only job that I could find in my field was a graveyard-shift counseling position working with developmentally disabled adults. What a let down!

After three months of trying to piece together a living, in hopes that we would be able to earn enough to get back out on our own, it became obvious that that job was going nowhere in a hurry. So, with limited options and a lack of assurance as to what God had in mind, I determined to find a way out. The only open door that came my way was to join the United States Army. I had been promised I would go into the Officer Candidate School and become an Army officer. I thought, "What a marvelous idea!" I'd been an athlete most of my life and I felt like this would be a piece of cake. Oh, was I wrong! What a difficult time that was for me and my wife. The Lord used it to the fullest measure as I learned the tactics of warfare, how to administrate, how to handle budgets, and how to manage personnel. This has been helpful in my pastoral and counseling ministries and business career. At the time, my future in ministry remained unclear. If I would have known the trails I would face, or I probably would not have taken this plunge. But I would not have received the training that has been used so effectively by God (paid for by the U.S. Government!).

59

In the midst of this crisis or transition time, I felt the gamut of emotions. I was initially angry at the Christian employer who I felt had lied to me. I felt hurt and abandoned by people that had said they would help me if I ever had a need. I felt somewhat lost, in that I wasn't sure what I was doing with my life. At times I was even disgruntled with God, wondering why He had allowed this situation to happen to me. Not very theologically astute, but at least I was honest in my emotions. Yet, I know for certain that God had His hand on my life throughout this process.

As we face crises in our careers, it is important that we keep our eyes open for what God might be doing in the midst of it. The Lord does want us to prosper, even as our soul prospers. God wants us to do the very best we can and be the best that we can be, in our careers and in all other aspects of life. As you seek after the Lord with all your heart, God will guide and direct your steps.

In the midst of a career crisis, it is important to remember the following things:

1. Realize that any career is only temporary. Eventually, all of us will retire one way or another. Remember, it is your employer's privilege to pay you as a member of the kingdom of God.

2. Keep a good family support system. All jobs are tentative; even the most secure can be taken away from you based upon economic changes, the works of the devil, etc. It is important that you have a solid support system both in your family and in the body of Christ. This can mean the difference between a great depression and just a depressing period of life.

3. Keep things in proper perspective. Rather than looking at your career as the most important area of your life, see it for what it is: a job. It is an avocation, not your vocation. Your primary vocation as a Christian is to make disciples. That should be the primary focus of all of our

lives as well as to build up the body of Christ and extend God's kingdom.

Any loss of a job or a major career change can cause certain symptoms to develop especially, anxiety and depression. By the grace of God, and by keeping our eyes fixed upon Jesus, the author and finisher of our faith, we will be able to run our race with endurance, and be able to complete the task that God has given to us.

"Therefore, since we are surrounded by such a great cloud of witnesses, let us throw off everything that hinders and the sin that so easily entangles, and let us run with perseverance the race marked out for us. Let us fix our eyes on Jesus, the author and perfecter of our faith, who for the joy set before him endured the cross, scorning its shame, and sat down at the right hand of the throne of God" (Hebrews 12:1-2)

Chapter 4

Adult Crises

Mid-life Crisis

Sally and Jim Conway have written some excellent books in the area of mid-life transitions and the empty nest syndrome. I will not go into great detail about these here, but it is important for us to recognize that there are transition times in men's and women's lives where crises can occur. However, crisis does not have to occur in the midst of midlife evaluation and change.

For men especially, mid-life transition occurs between the ages of 38 and 45. It is a time when they re-evaluate where they are in life, career, relationship, and what they want to do with the rest of their lives. Most men will take a look back over the previous ten years in order to judge how successful they have been in comparison to their goals and values. If they have done well, they tend to transition smoothly. If they have not accomplished certain important goals, or feel as if they have been cheated in some way by life, they may experience their "growing older" as a significant crisis. Further, men begin to recognize that the joys and strengths of youth are beginning to wane. Thus, you may observe men who run out to buy a Porsche, put gold chains around their neck, divorce their wives and find a younger woman in their search for youth and vitality. Their panic is designed to somehow chase away the fear of coming death and embrace life again. It is a sadly chosen delusion.

The Word of God indicates that we do not need to fear death. Death has no sting, no power over us. As Christians, we are to live our lives in an appropriate way, continuing to follow God's covenant. We do not have to be subject to the media driven pressures of life. We can overcome by the power of God.

This time of transition, is a time to re-evaluate. "Who am I? What am I all about? What should I be doing with the rest of my life?" It is a time of change.

Thankfully, we have energy to make changes. This is an opportunity to make necessary mid-course corrections for the betterment of self and others. It is important for men to recognize these transition times and the church must help them to recognize new choices can be made.

Empyt Nest Syndrome

The empty nest syndrome for most women corresponds with men's mid-life transition, at approximately the time that the children begin to leave home. This is especially difficult for women who have invested their entire life in the care of their children. It is also difficult if their relationship with their spouse has not been a healthy one. Much of a woman's identity can be wrapped up in the role of "mother." They may forget that their primary responsibility is to God first, then to their spouse. When children depart the home, a loss of the sense of self worth can lead to crisis. This can include symptoms of depression, anxiety, and other forms of psychological malady.

For most women it is important to recognize that their value and worth is not based upon what they do but upon who they are in relationship to the Lord Jesus Christ. Women have great value, position, and importance in the body of Christ. Assisting women, who are transitioning their children to adulthood, is a ministry of the local church that can be most beneficial.

The Latter Years

The Word of God indicates that those with gray hair, or men and women in their later years, are to be shown honor or respect. It is assumed that with age comes the impartation of the wisdom and knowledge that has been gained through life experience. In Western culture, we tend to put people out to pasture when they reach their latter years. This is a travesty, which should never occur especially within the church. I remember, as a young teen spending many hours with my great uncle and my grandfather, talking to them about their lives and the interesting things that they had experienced. I was able to gain valuable knowledge and wisdom from them because I was willing to listen. We need to respect our elders and treat them with love and kindness so that they are able to fulfill their role during the golden years.

"Few things are more satisfying than seeing your own children have teenagers of their own."
- Doug Larson

"Like its politicians and its wars, society has the teenagers it deserves."
- J.B. Priestly

SECTION 2

Situational Crisis

Introduction

By in large, a situational crisis is one which cannot be controlled. It is essentially being in the wrong place at the wrong time. Of course, as you review many of the "situations" presented here, some situational crises are chosen, some thrust upon us. However the crisis comes, with God and good counsel, crisis can often be circumvented, controlled, and resolved.

Chapter 5

Substance Abuse in Adolescents

What is substance abuse[5]? Drug abuse, which includes alcohol abuse, can be defined as the use of any chemical substance that causes physical, emotional, or social harm to a person or to people close to him or her.

In the United States, the level of drug and alcohol abuse among young people is the highest of any developed country in the world. At present there are an estimated 3.3 million teenagers who would be classified as alcoholics. Nearly two-thirds of our youth have tried an illicit drug at some time before they have graduated from high school. Many children who are into heavy drugs by the age of 17 have started as early as age 11. One-third of all suicides, regardless of age, are alcohol related. National estimates of the annual cost to the United States because of drug abuse and alcoholism is over 100 billion dollars.

What are some of the causes of substance abuse and how can we deal with it?

1. Family problems. In a chemically dependent family, members may unknowingly encourage drinking or drug behavior. Certainly, every member of the family becomes involved in the alcohol or drug abuse dysfunction and in the dysfunction of the dependent person. There are certain names that have been given to the roles that people will play in order to attempt to cope with the alcohol and drug abuse problem. They have best been developed by Virginia Satir, a well-known psychotherapist and educator. They include:

   a) The enabler. Often the spouse or parent, though it can be one of the children. The enabler is usually the one the substance abuser depends upon the most. This family member becomes more and more responsible for the family to make up for the

71

lack of control of the substance abuser or the lack of input into the family.

b) The family hero. This individual is especially sensitive to the needs of the family. They feel responsible for its pain. The hero does every thing possible to improve the situation by trying to present him or herself as a success in the environment outside the home.

c) The scapegoat. This individual does not work as hard as the hero to achieve recognition; but instead, pulls away in a destructive manner by getting into trouble, hurting themselves or withdrawing. In doing this they attempt to bring the attention of the family away from the substance abuser and onto themselves.

d) The lost child. This child offers relief to the family by taking care of personal problems and avoiding trouble. The family ignores the child who is then left to face problems all alone. In many cases this child is the one who suffers the most pain within the family while seeming to be the least affected.

e) The mascot. This person provides relief for the family through humor. By being the "class clown" they mask their own pain and loneliness for the sake of what seems to be the family good.

What interventions are available to assist the family?

a) Intervention is designed to motivate the abuser to seek help. Without help, whether through intervention by the Spirit of God (a tremendous conversion experience), or through the loving support of a family, the abuser is likely to continue to abuse drugs as a way to meet their desperate needs. If an intervention occurs, it should be done under the supervision of a pastor or a trained counselor who understands how to develop an intervention process.

b) Treatment. I have said many times, "The most normal, well-integrated human being that does not know Christ, is just as readily going to hell as one that is a total mess." With that in mind, I believe it is essential for a substance abuser to come to know Christ as their personal Savior. They need the empowerment of the Holy Spirit if they are going to be able to overcome the temptations of the devil and to be able to walk in victory over their substance abuse problem.

c) Along with treatment, most substance abusers, especially teenagers, must learn how to re-socialize themselves. In most cases they have had very little or poor parenting. They need to re-learn how to live their lives in a more appropriate manner. This is where 12- step groups, such as developed by Alcoholics Anonymous but in a Christian vein, counseling services, home groups and outreaches may help to reintegrate the individual substance abuser and teach them how to live a healthy Christian life.

d) There is certainly no substitute for learning the Word of God and applying it to their lives. They need a strict and disciplined approach because they have learned to be very undisciplined and self-absorbed. The counselor involved with a substance abuser must be wary and use wisdom in ministering to them.

Chapter 6

Eating Disorders

There are tremendous pressures placed upon adolescent females to be, as it were, perfect. Compounding media driven pressure is the myth of perfection within Western culture; that we cannot be accepted unless we are razor thin, have perfect straight teeth, gorgeous hair, and an IQ of 160. Of course, we all know that reality is quite different. Yet, to a teenager, trying to fit in, trying to be a part of the group, to be seen as worthwhile and okay among their peers is of vital importance.

One disorder or crisis that is occurring all too often amongst adolescents, including in the evangelical Christian world, is that of eating disorders. I will define them here and give a brief description of how to deal with the eating disorder problem within our society.

What are the eating disorders and the counseling issues related to them?

1.   Bulimia and Anorexia. These are two bingeing and starving disorders that afflict thousands of adolescent and young adult women. One of the most famous cases of this was that of Karen Carpenter, the singer who died from heart problems caused by anorexia nervosa. The characteristics of these disorders and the psychological family profile of the victims are very important and are described here.

    a) Bulimia is a recurrent episode of binge eating followed by awareness that the eating pattern is abnormal, and accompanies a fear of being unable to stop voluntarily. This is followed by a depressed mood and self-deprecating thoughts of guilt and severe anxiety.

        The majority of bulimics binge in secret and resort to self-induced

75

vomiting, or purging. At first glance, this disorder may sound a 20th/21st Century invention; however it dates back to the Roman days of orgies, gorging, and then vomiting. A typical binge episode averages over 4,000 calories, lasts for as much as an hour, and occurs up to twice a day. The damage that is physically done in bulimics is tremendous and therefore there is a great need for medical, as well as psychological and physical care.

b) Anorexia is, first of all, characterized by a 25% weight loss, or a body weight that is 25% below normal. Secondly there is an intense fear of becoming obese. Thirdly, the victim experiences a distorted body image. When they look at themselves in the mirror, they see themselves as fat, or just right, when they are clearly emaciated. There is a refusal to maintain weight above the minimum norm for their age and height.

Anorexics may also binge and purge, and will frequently abuse physical exercise to excess. Usually they suffer from more severe psychological and medical problems than will bulimics.

Bulimia and anorexia are quite extensive within Western Culture. It is estimated that there are from half a million to five million bulimics and anorexics in the United States. This estimate includes up to 13% of the adolescent and young adult female population as bulimics, and 11% as anorexics.

What is the psychosocial profile of this eating disordered individual? The typical image is that of a model child, the perfect little princess. Behind this is a very poor self-image, a tremendous need for approval, especially from parents, and a compulsion for high achievement. Most of these adolescents also see any form of flaw within their character or body image as a distinct failure, which they assume will invite rejection from those that care about them. Because of this they have an obsessive sense of anxiety or fear which dominates their life experience.

Further, a woman's social dependency in culture many times idealizes thin bodies. In this view, dependency defines females in terms of other than self, making them highly responsive to external demands or rewards. They are then unable to find internal sources of rewards.

The families of most anorexics and bulimics are typically dependant on each other and cannot handle stress and anger in a positive way. They are enmeshed, that is they are overly concerned and overly involved in each other's lives, and no clear boundaries between individuals are found. Paradoxically, the eating disorder functions to preserve family stability. The victim secures a sense of identity, approval and control through the special attention she receives because of the illness. This requires everyone else to be involved in her life and illness and assists them in avoiding the real family conflicts that do exist.

How does one deal with this crisis? As with many problems, you must first confront the denial that exists within the family system. Recently, I was working with a young lady who had been bulimic and anorexic for a number of years. Even after she had been entered into a specialized treatment center (she was near death due to her bulimia), her parents would talk to her in terms of the idealized child, not able to recognize how debilitating the disease really was. She was literally killing herself as a way to keep the family focused on her and avoid dealing with their own problems.

After confronting the denial, it is very important to recognize that a multi-disciplinary approach is needed. There must be physical needs met through nutrition and sometimes pervasive medical care. There needs to be individual counseling, family counseling, and sometimes group counseling.

When good treatment occurs, and especially when the power of the Holy Spirit is introduced into an individual's life, over 80% will eventually become binge/purge free. There is a significantly higher success rate in those that come to know Christ over those who do not, showing that the power of the Holy Spirit is necessary to break what, I believe, can be a spiritual or demonic manifestation in many. It most likely does not start that way, but it becomes a stronghold in a teenager's life that can only be broken by the power of almighty God. We must realize that once the power is broken, there is a need for continuing care, discipleship, and training to assist the young person to overcome this debilitating disorder.

Chapter 7

Teenage Pregnancy

Teenage pregnancy and parenthood has been a major social issue for many years in Western Nations. There are currently large numbers of young women in the thirteen to nineteen age range who become pregnant annually. There are major decisions that must be made during this time of crisis. As Christians, we hold strongly to the belief in the sanctity of life; therefore, abortion is not an option for Christian teenagers. We would like to say it is not an option for the non-Christian as well, yet the pressures to have an abortion are prevelant. That leaves the possibility of either adoption, and all the subsequent problems that occur because of that, or keeping the child, with the difficulties that occur there. No easy choices come with teen pregnancy.

What are some of the ways that we can avoid the possibility of teenage pregnancy? First of all, especially with the onset of AIDS and all the problems of socially transmitted diseases, it is important that the church be willing to teach and train their young people a positive view of human sexuality. Josh McDowell, in his book and tape series, *Why Wait?*, has done a tremendous job in giving our young people reasons why they should wait before having sexual relations in the teenage years. That is, there are tremendous blessings to gain from waiting until marriage to be sexually involved. The peer pressure that is upon young people, the pressure to be a part of the group, the pressure to experience the exhilaration of sexual relations is tremendous. It is very important that we assist our teenagers by being open and candid, and teaching them what the Word of God says about human sexuality, marriage, and family relations.

How do we respond if a teenager does become pregnant? Number one, it is important to remember we know what causes this! It should not be a tremendous shock. Without sexual intercourse it is pretty difficult for anyone to become pregnant. That is why teaching and training is needed beforehand. Secondly, it is not a disease, nor is the teenager any less of a human being because they have become pregnant. It is important that we do not respond with shock or rage, but that we deal with the teenager in a mature, and hopefully, grace-filled and loving manner.

Teenage parenthood is by no means a new social phenomenon. Historically, women have tended to begin their childbearing years during their teens or early twenties. During the past two plus decades in the U.S., teenage birthrate has actually declined (Potit et al., 1982). In the late 50's, 90 out of 1,000 women under 20 gave birth as compared with 52 out of 1,000 in 1978. Several factors contribute to the current attention focused on teenage pregnancy and parenthood.

1. There is currently a large number of young women in the 13 to 19 age range so that while the birthrates are declining, the absolute number of teenagers (and subsequently, teen's giving birth) is increasing.
2. These statistics do not distinguish between intentional and unintentional pregnancies, or pregnancies occurring in or out of wedlock. From 1978 figures, only one in six pregnancies concluded as births following marriage, and eight in ten premarital teenage pregnancies were unintended.
3. The declining birthrate is not consistent for all teenagers: among those 14 or younger, the birthrate is increasing.
4. These trends are occurring at a time when contraceptives are increasingly available to teenagers as a means of avoiding unwanted pregnancy.
5. The evidence documenting the unfavorable consequences of unintended teenage pregnancy and teenage parenthood has continued to mount.
6. There is an unmistakable and dramatic trend away from teenagers giving up their children for adoption.

Thus, the magnitude of the problem, together with its perceived costs and avoidability, have combined to make teenage pregnancy and parenthood a national social issue.

Teenage Pregnancy Rate

How Bad is the Problem?

- The United States has the highest rates of teen pregnancy and births in the western industrialized world. Teen pregnancy costs the United States at least $7 billion annually.
- Nearly four in ten young women become pregnant at least once before they reach the age of 20 – nearly one million a year. Eight in ten of these pregnancies are unintended and 79 percent are to unmarried teens.
- The teen birth rate has declined slowly but steadily from 1991 to 2001 with an overall decline of 27 percent for those aged 15 to 19. These recent declines reverse the 24-percent rise in the teenage birth rate from 1986 to 1991. The largest decline since 1991 by race was for black women. The birth rate for black teens aged 15 to 19 fell 38 percent between 1991 and 2001. Hispanic teen birth rates declined 20 percent between 1994 and 2001. The rates of both Hispanics and blacks, however, remain higher than for other groups. Hispanic teens now have the highest teenage birth rates. Most teenagers giving birth before 1980 were married whereas most teens giving birth today are unmarried.
- The younger a teenaged girl is when she has sex for the first time, the more likely she is to have had unwanted or non-voluntary sex. Close to four in ten girls who had first intercourse at 13 or 14 report it was either non-voluntary or unwanted.

Who suffers the consequences?

- Teen mothers are less likely to complete high school, (only on-third receive a high school diploma) and more likely to end up on welfare (nearly 80 percent of unmarried teen mothers end up on welfare).
- The children of teenage mothers have lower birth weights, are more likely to perform poorly in school, and are at greater risk of abuse and neglect.

81

- The sons of teen mothers are 13 percent more likely to end up in prison while teen daughters are 22 percent more likely to become teen mothers themselves.

What helps prevent teen pregnancy?

- The primary reason that teenage girls who have never had intercourse give for abstaining from sex is that having sex would be against their religious or moral values. Other reasons cited include desire to avoid pregnancy, fear of contracting a sexually transmitted disease (STD), and not having met the appropriate partner. Three of four girls and over half of boys report that girls who have sex do so because their boyfriends want them to.
- Teenagers who have strong emotional attachments to their parents are much less likely to become sexually active at an early age.
- Most people say teens should remain abstinent but should have access to contraception. Ninety-five percent of adults in the United States – and 85 percent of teenagers – think it important that school-aged children and teenagers be given a strong message from society that they should abstain from sex until they are out of high school. Almost 60 percent of adults also think that sexually active teenagers should have access to contraception.
- Contraception use among sexually active teens has increased but remains inconsistent. Three-quarters of teens use some method of contraception (usually a condom) the first time they have sex. A sexually active teen who does not use contraception has a 90 percent chance of pregnancy within one year.
- Parents rate high among many teens as trustworthy and preferred information sources on birth control. One in two teens say they "trust" their parents most for reliable and complete information about birth control, only 12 percent say a friend.
- Teens who have been raised by both parents (biological or adoptive) from birth, have lower probabilities of having sex than teens who grew up in any other family situation. At age 16, 22 percent of girls from intact families and 44 percent of other girls have had sex at least once.

82

Similarly, teens from intact, two-parent families are less likely to give birth in their teens than girls from other family backgrounds.

When should I talk to my child about sex?

- Before they make you a grandparent. One of every three girls has had sex by age 16, two out of three by age 18. Two of 3 boys have had sex by age 18.
- Surprise: Your teen wants to hear from you. Seven of ten teens interviewed said that they were ready to listen to things parents thought they were not ready to hear. When asked about the reasons why teenage girls have babies, 78 percent of white and 70 percent of African-American teenagers reported that lack of communication between a girl and her parents is often a reason teenage girls have babies.

Do teens wish they had waited to have sex?

- Yes. A majority of both girls and boys who are sexually active wish they had waited. Eight in ten girls and six in ten boys say they wish they had waited until they were older to have sex.

Teenage Birthrate

About five percent of U.S. teenagers give birth each year. A study by the Alan Guttmacher Institute showed teen birthrates here to be twice as high as Canada, England and Wales, three times as high as Sweden, and seven times higher than the Netherlands.

Out of Wedlock Births

Although slowed because of the availability of legal abortion, the rise in out of wedlock birthrate has continued among almost all groups of teenagers. The rise has been steepest among 15-17 year old whites. The number of premarital births legitimated by marriage has been declining.

Adoption and Care by Others

Almost all unwed teenage mothers keep their children in the household with them. Ninety-six percent of unmarried teenage mothers, 90% of white and nearly all black mothers, keep their children with them (although in many cases grandparents or other relatives help with the care of the baby).

Repeated Unintentional Pregnancies

As might be expected, 78% of births to teenagers are first births. However, 19% are second births, and 4% are third or higher order births. The sooner the teenager gives birth after the initiation of intercourse, the more likely she is to have subsequent births while still in her teens.

Though these stats are of the United States, similar percentages can be found in other Western Nations worldwide.

Teenage Contraception

Provided here are the standard secular (non-evangelical Christian) response to teenage sexual activity. The rational for contraceptive usage is presented for informational purposes, though not endorsed by the author.

Nearly two-thirds of unwed teenage women report that they never practice contraception or that they use a method inconsistently. According to the Guttmacher Institute (Teenage Pregnancy 1981), only 9% of unmarried teenagers surveyed said that they did not use a method of contraception because they were trying to become pregnant or were already intentionally pregnant. Forty-one percent thought they could not become pregnant, mainly because they believed, usually mistakenly, that it was the wrong time of the month. Of those who had realized that they could get pregnant, the major reason given for not using a method was that they had not expected to have intercourse. Of those who did not practice because they were pregnant, the overwhelming majority were pregnant unintentionally. About 8% said that they had wanted to use a method but "couldn't under the circumstances," or that they did not know about contraception, nor where to get it.

Relationship to Pregnancy

The relationship between pregnancy and contraceptive use is dramatic: about 62% of sexually active teenagers who have never used a method have experienced a pre-marital pregnancy, compared to 30% of those who have used a method inconsistently, 14% of those who have always used some method (including withdrawal) and just 7% of those who have always used a medically prescribed method (the pill, IUD, or diaphragm).

In 1976, teenagers experienced about 780,000 premarital pregnancies. It has been estimated that if no contraceptives had been used, there would have been nearly double the amount of teenage pregnancies.

The Health Belief Model

Meanwhile, many teenagers remain non-users or inconsistent users of contraceptives. Reasons for this vary widely, from lack of knowledge, to psychological factors, such as inability to see themselves as sexual, lack of planning, egocentric thinking, or the influence of religious beliefs and values. Current research has examined the Health Belief Model (Zellman, 1984), a value expectancy approach to explaining and predicting health behaviors that goes beyond straightforward information giving. This approach can be used to intervene in contraceptive use among teenagers. Because contraceptive action involves the prevention health decision followed by correct and consistent use, the model may have used application to both the prevention and compliance aspects of contraceptive behavior.

Sex Education

The subject of sex education remains a diverse one. On one side there are those who argue that Americans should learn to accept adolescent sexuality and make guidance and birth control more easily available, as it is in parts of

85

Europe. On the other side there are those who contend that sex education is up to the parents, not the state, and that teaching children about birth control is tantamount to condoning promiscuity, or violating family religious beliefs and values. Certainly, the later position is the one most espoused in Christian homes, though not always the one practiced.

Sex Education in the Schools

Eight out of ten Americans believe that sex education should be taught in the schools, and seven out of ten believe that such courses should include information about contraception (Teenage Pregnancy, 1981, p. 38). Only a handful of states require or even encourage sex education, and fewer still encourage teaching about birth control or abortion. Most states leave the question of sex education up to the local school boards. Only a minority, however, provide such instruction.

Parents and Sex Education

Parents are a child's earliest models of sexuality; they communicate with their children about sex and sexual values non-verbally. However, most adolescents report that they have never been given any advice about sex even though a majority of teenagers prefer their parents and counselors as sources of sex information.

Studies indicate that both parents and their children believe that they should be talking about sexuality, but that parents are extremely uncomfortable doing so (Sexuality Education, 1984). Organizations, including churches, schools, and other agencies, serving young people, offer programs designed to help parents teach their children about sexuality. Most would agree that sex education should start early, before a child's sexuality becomes an issue.

Family Planning Services

Most teenagers and adults approve of making contraceptives available to teenagers and most parents favor family planning clinics providing birth control services to their children (Teenage Pregnancy, 1981). Although this obviously contradicts our Christian beliefs, it is important to understand our world's perspective. However, most teenagers are sexually active for many months before ever seeking birth control help from a family planning clinic or physician (Teenage Pregnancy, 1981). Very few come to a clinic in anticipation of initiating sexual intercourse, and many come because they fear, often correctly, that they are already pregnant. The major reason teenagers give for the delay is concern that their parents will find out about the visit. Nevertheless, more than half of teenage patients have told their parents about their clinic visit, and only about one quarter would not come if the clinic required parental notification. But most of these would continue to be sexually active, using less effective methods or no contraceptives and many thousands would get pregnant as a result.

Solving the Problem

Although we have most of the knowledge and resources needed to solve the problem of teenage pregnancy, we have failed to do so. Despite the growing public concern and the plethora of reports, there has been little action. The elements of a comprehensive, national program have been put forward, with varying emphases, by a number of groups. Elements of such programs include: (Teenage Pregnancy, 1981)

1. Realistic sex education (Why Wait?, Josh McDowell)
2. An expanded network of preventive family planning services
3. Pregnancy counseling services from a Christian perspective
4. Adequate prenatal, obstetric and pediatric care and loving ministry for teenage mothers and their children
5. Educational, employment and social services for adolescent parents
6. Coverage by national health insurance of all health services related to teenage pregnancy and childbearing
7. Return to solid Christian family values

No one program can possibly solve the many problems that are associated with teenage pregnancy. The solution must come from elements of society:

87

parents, the churches, the schools, state and local legislatures and government agencies. Most people agree about the importance of finding solutions and services for teenagers, but there is not yet the willingness to pay the costs for such programs in most communities.

Chapter 8

Suicide

Joanne sat nervously as Melody drove her into town toward Community Hospital. The drive seemed to take forever, although it took only ten minutes. At the moment, it seemed like an eternity since she had climbed into the car. She really didn't know what to expect when she got to the hospital, but she knew from the tone of the nurse who had called her that it was a very serious problem. She had received the emergency call while she was at work and there wasn't the time to ask a lot of questions. All that she knew was that her son, Josh, had been shot and she was needed at the hospital at once.

Joanne was a teacher's aid at Bridgeport Elementary School and was in the process of giving basic tests in the classroom when she was startled by hearing her name called over the intercom: "Joanne Taylor, you have an emergency telephone call in the office." Joanne knew it had to be an emergency since staff members were rarely called out of the classroom. She made her way down the long hallway, wondering which one of her kids was sick now.

Joanne had two children, Josh, age 17, and Judy, age 15, and it seemed like one of them was always getting a severe cold, or the flu, or having an accident. Something was always going on with them. However, both Josh and Judy were very strong individuals and there was never any reason to really worry about them. She was grateful because they were both very popular and achieved grades well above average. Josh, especially, was very conscious about his grades and was always on the honor roll at school. They both seemed very sure of themselves and seemed to be very happy.

She finally reached the office and picked up the receiver of the phone; "Hello, this is Mrs. Taylor."

"Hello, Mrs. Taylor, this is the head nurse at Community Hospital. I'm sorry to tell you this, but your son Joshua has been brought into the hospital with a gunshot wound. Can you please come to the hospital immediately?"

Joanne managed a frail, "Of course, I'll be right there."

Joanne's friend, Melody, had been standing there beside Joanne and knew immediately that something was terribly wrong. "Joanne, what's the matter?"

"It's Josh, he's been shot, and I've got to get to the hospital right away." Melody dropped everything she had been doing, quickly punched both of them out on the time clock, put her arm around the shoulder of Joanne and said, "Come on, I'll take you to the hospital so you won't have to drive."

The trip seemed long, but they finally reached the emergency room door of Community Hospital. Joanne walked up to the desk and told the nurse who she was and asked if she could see her son, Josh. "I'll get Dr. Donald," the nurse replied. "He does want to talk to you first. Please be seated, he'll be right with you." Within minutes, Dr. Donald was coming down the hall.

Dr. Donald had a very distinguished appearance and just one look at the tall, handsome, elderly gentleman commanded respect and trust. Joanne knew that he was a Christian man and a true man of faith.

"Hello, Mrs. Taylor, please come into my office, it will be better if we talk there." Slowly Joanne and Melody followed the doctor to his office deeply sensing that something was terribly wrong. "Please, doctor, tell me how Josh is, I have to know! When can I see him? Is he conscious? How bad is it?"

"Mrs. Taylor, please sit down here on the couch, we have to talk first."

Impatiently, Joanne and Melody sat down on the couch. Dr. Donald sat down beside Joanne and gently took her hand in his. "I'm sorry Mrs. Taylor, we did everything that we could possibly do, but your son died just a few minutes ago." Joanne, stunned and in shock, began to cry.

"I've got to see him, please let me see him." Dr. Donald was gentle and caring, and his voice was quiet and low. "Mrs. Taylor, there is something else you have to know, before you see him. You see, Josh died of a self-inflicted gun shot wound to the head. This note was found beside him."

Joanne tearfully and nervously took the note in her hand and fearfully opened the folded piece of paper. Her shoulders sank and her heart broke as she read these words: "I'm sorry, Mom and Dad, please don't cry for me, I must do this, Good-bye." Joanne collapsed into Dr. Donald's arms sobbing uncontrollably. "Why, why? He seemed so happy and content. Why? What could have possibly happened to make him do it?"

Suicide...the very word sends sharp pains of emotion through those whose lives it has touched. Unfortunately Joanne, and many other parents like her, may never know the real reason why their children choose to take their own lives. Their reasons are as varied as the young people themselves. Suicide is always accompanied by the question, "WHY? Did I do something wrong? What could we have done differently?" And the questions go on and on. Unfortunately, sometimes it is accompanied by accusations to the other family members or friends that only serve to drive deep wedges of blame and hurt between our loved ones.

Taken from Professional Exchange, The California Therapist, November December 2001, Sharmil Shah, MA author

According to the American Academy of Pediatrics, "Suicide is the third leading cause of death for adolescents fifteen to nineteen years old." The suicide rate has increased by 300 percent from 1950-1990. (American Academy of Pediatrics, 2000).

Before reviewing the causes and treatment, including prevention of Teen Suicide (and suicide in general) there are Fifteen Prevalent Myths Concerning Adolescent Suicide, presented by Sharmil Shah. They are:

1. Adolescent Suicide is a decreasing problem in the United States (King, 1999). This is absolutely untrue. As stated above, the suicide rate for adolescents has increased 300 percent.

2. Homicide is more prevalent than suicide in adolescents. Actually, homicide is the third leading cause of death among youth; second to suicide.

3. Suicide occurs without warning signs. Most suicide attempts are a cry for help, and statistically, nine out of ten adolescents who do commit suicide give clues to others beforehand.

4. Adolescents who talk about suicide do not commit suicide. One of the most important warning signs is the repeated discussion of one's death. All threats should be taken seriously.

5. Adolescents who attempt suicide want to die. A suicide attempt is a cry for help. There is confusion on the part of the adolescent regarding whether to stay in their pain of continue living with no hope.

6. Education about suicide will only increase the rate of suicide. Talking about suicide does not increase the likelihood of it occurring, but lessens it.

7. Other adolescents cannot relate to a person with suicidal thoughts. The fact is, over 40% of teen's contemplated suicide at least once in their lives.

8. There are no differences between males and females when it comes to suicide. Males are more likely to complete a suicide, whereas females are more likely to have thought about it.

9.   Since the rate of female suicides is lower than males, they should not be taken as seriously. Of course, all threats should be taken seriously.

10.   The most common method for youth suicide is drug overdose. The fact is, firearms are the leading method, followed by pill ingestion.

11.   All adolescents who engage in suicidal behavior are mentally ill. Some adolescents are suffering from mental disorders, but many are not. Their suffering is from a live disorder (difficult environment, child abuse, sexual abuse, etc.).

12.   There is nothing one can do if an adolescent wants to commit suicide. Education about the warning signs and risk factors are the best ways to prevent a suicide.

13.   Suicidal behavior is inherited. Although prior family history of suicide is a risk factor, there is not definitive proof that there is a suicidal gene.

14.   Suicide only occurs among the poor. Socioeconomic status is not a valid predictor for suicide.

15.   Only mental health professional can help a suicidal adolescent. More often, doctors, peer counselors, and school officials (along with informed church families) are getting involved in the care of suicidal adolescents. Their main responsibility is to refer the adolescent to a mental health professional.

Identification, Intervention, and Prevention

The teenage suicide rate has risen to crisis proportions over the past 20 years. Between 1957 and 1975, the rate of suicide among 15-24 year olds tripled; among Native American adolescents, the suicide rate increased 1000%

(Teenagers in Crisis, 1983). It is estimated that 5,000 to 6,000 teenagers kill themselves each year, and at least ten times that many attempt to do so. Amongst the U.S. population, according to the Center for Disease Control, 2001, there were a total of 30, 575 confirmed suicides. Suicide is highest among people age 65 and older and the leading cause of death for people ages 15-24. More people die from suicide than homicide each year, making suicide the 8th leading cause of death in America. Because many suicide attempts go unreported as accidents, the estimated number may be as high as 500,000 per year. While females attempt suicide more often than males, at a rate of 4:1, males "succeed" more often, at the same rate (Suicide Among School Age Youth, 1984).

The rising rate has been explained as a reaction to the stress inherent in adolescence compounded by increasing stress in the environment. Adolescence is a time of stress heightened by physical, psychological, emotional, and social changes. Adolescents suffer a feeling of loss for the childhood they must leave behind, and undergo a difficult period of adjustment to their new adult identity.

Our achievement-oriented, highly competitive society puts pressure on teens to succeed, often forcing them to set unrealistically high, personal expectations. In an affluent society, which emphasizes immediate rewards, adolescents are not taught to be tolerant of frustration. Blurred gender roles can also be confusing and frustrating for teens (Rosenkrantz,1978).

Some researchers attribute teenage suicide to the weakening of the family unit. It is no longer able to supply family members with a sense of stability and rootedness (Suicide and Attempted Suicide, 1974). Awareness of the existing state of the world, now threatened by sophisticated methods of destruction, can cause depression which contributes to the adolescent's sense of frustration, helplessness, and hopelessness (Smith, 1979). Faced with these feelings and lacking coping mechanisms adolescents can become overwhelmed and turn to escapist measures such as drugs, withdrawal, and ultimately, suicide.

Suicide is not an impulsive act but the result of a three step process:

1. A previous history of problems
2. Problems associated with adolescence
3. A precipitating event

Problems can create further difficulties for the adolescent, causing social isolation and withdrawal, poor school performance and attendance, and repeated suicide attempts. The precipitating event, which triggers a suicide attempt, is usually a family crisis, a significant personal loss, or an upset to self-esteem (such as failing a course, losing one's place on a sport's team, or being fired from a part time job). The anniversary of a loss can also evoke a powerful desire to commit suicide (Frederick, 1976)

A teen at risk of committing suicide is experiencing deep depression, which may be indicated by a loss of weight, appetite or interest in personal appearance. A change in sleeping pattern, fatigue, and feelings of hopelessness and low self esteem may be evident. Sudden behavioral changes may occur. The youth may become disruptive, violent, or hostile toward family and friends; or unexplainably moody, suspicious, anxious, or selfish. He or she may spend a great deal of time daydreaming, fantasizing, or imagining ills, in extreme cases experiencing memory lapses or hallucinations.

The teenager may express a desire to die, threaten to commit suicide, or inform friends of a plan. Self-abusive acts such as cutting off hair and self-inflicted cigarette burns are obvious suicidal gestures. The teen may develop a preoccupation with death and dying, make arrangements to give away prized possessions, withdraw from therapeutic help, or rapidly lose interest in once-valued activities and objects.

Peer pressure is often a very real and serious conflict in a young person's life. Every day they have to answer questions that will affect, in some way or the other, the future and the quality of their life.

Drugs and alcohol are persistent temptations that lure young people. But they are only part of the turmoil and inner struggles our youth are faced with.

In dealing with crisis, it is often difficult to admit that easy solutions are rare. Facing up to the realities at hand may also require admitting that resolving the crisis may be painful in a variety of ways. In fact, solutions may just possibly be more painful for you as parents, than for your teen. The trials and tribulations of the early going may be especially distressing, but may be a necessary path towards resolution.

Warning Signs

There are certain signs that mental health experts have isolated as warning signals that may indicate suicidal tendencies. Listed below are some of the most common things to look for.

1. Radical personality changes such as persistent sadness, loss of interest in usual activities, feelings of guilt, worthlessness and helplessness
2. Impulsive behavior (He rebels and refuses to talk to anybody about the problems he may be going through at the time.)
3. Inability to tolerate frustrations. This translates into wanting everything here and now. They expect instant answers, instant pleasures, and instant results. He has an inability to tolerate frustrations and he cannot get along with others around him. Parents and teachers sometimes relate this behavior to being selfish and petulant.
4. Withdrawal from family, friends and regular activities. There may be extreme changes in peer relationships. Even the teen who maintained a good relationship with parents, teens and teachers, may suddenly reject both family and teachers. He may sever all significant ties. (This is what happened to Josh.)
5. Noticeable changes in eating or sleeping habits or energy levels; sometimes he will neglect his personal appearance.
6. Falling grades in school (Academic problems that never existed before)
7. Difficulty in concentrating
8. Violent or rebellious behavior. This may include a sudden mistrust of all adults. He may have a severe resistance to adult-imposed regulations. He will assume that adults cannot be trusted and that you certainly cannot confide in adults.

96

9. Drug and alcohol abuse
10. Physical symptoms often related to emotional disturbances, such as stomach, headache, or fatigue
11. Thoughts expressed of despair, death or suicide. Be attentive to the teen's feeling and saying that one is hopeless or worthless.
12. Suicide attempts, even those that are meant to fail
13. Verbal hints or statements such as, "I won't be a problem for you much longer," and, "Nothing matters anymore." LISTEN for all verbal statements about running away or suicides. Many teens will use running away as a suicidal gesture.
14. Teens may begin to put their affairs in order. They will begin to give away some of their favorite possessions, throw things out, and make sure there is nothing out of place in their room.
15. He may suddenly become cheerful after prolonged depression, the final decision has been made, which in itself is a form of relief.
16. Feelings of a desire for revenge against a former girlfriend or boyfriend or other offending person
17. Magical thinking. This clearly signals a break with reality, and an inability to deal with pressures.

Parents must understand the cumulative nature of stress and its impact on teens. They must admit to the existence of problems, when they occur and confront them at the time. Explore options for solutions and don't be afraid to get outside help if needed. It is of major importance to include the teen in the solution process. Listen and talk non-combatively; with an open heart.

There seems to be universal agreement on the manner in which to counsel suicidal teens:

1. Be non-judgmental.
2. Treat the youth's problems seriously, and take all threats seriously.
3. Do not try to talk the person out of it.
4. Ask direct questions, such as, "Have you been thinking of killing yourself?" Don't be afraid that you will be suggesting

97

something the adolescent has not yet considered; usually your mentioning the topic is a relief.

5. Communicate your concern and support.
6. Offer yourself as a caring listener until professional help can be arranged.
7. Try to evaluate the seriousness of the risk, in order to make the appropriate referral to a health care professional, counselor, or concerned teacher.
8. Do not swear to secrecy. Contact someone who can help the adolescent if he or she will not do it personally.
9. Do not leave the person alone if you feel the threat is immediate.

In a counseling situation, a contract can be an effective prevention technique. Once past the crisis, follow up is crucial, because most suicides occur within three months of the beginning of improvement, when the youth has the energy to carry out plans conceived earlier.

Community members, mental health professionals, school personnel, peers, and parents can play major roles in the prevention of teenage suicide. Programs that build adolescent's self-esteem and inspire a sense of inclusion in, rather than alienation from, society have been found to be particularly effective. Churches and other religious communities can sponsor suicide prevention programs, and engage youth in the planning and implementation of programs for aiding the elderly, working in day care centers, training peer counselors and improving the environment.

Mental health personnel can educate students, counselors, teachers, and others, such as nurses and religious youth group leaders, in suicide identification and prevention. They can lead crisis-intervention workshops for counselors and teachers and train peer counselors in the middle and high schools. They can establish suicide crisis centers with telephone hotlines, support groups, outreach teams to facilitate grief groups for families and in schools, and research facilities for further study.

Teachers play an especially important part in prevention, because they spend so much time with their students. Along with holding parent-teacher meetings to discuss teenage suicide prevention, teachers can form networks with mental health professionals.

Peers are crucial to suicide prevention. According to one survey, 93% of the students reported that they would turn to a friend before a teacher, parent, or spiritual guide in time of crisis (Teenagers in Crisis, 1983).

Finally, parents need to be as open and as attentive as possible to their adolescent children's difficulties. The most effective suicide prevention technique parents can exercise is to maintain open lines of communication with their children.

There are many types of problems that today's youth encounter. For example:

1. Sex and facts of life
2. Drugs and alcohol.
3. School days and it's new problems
4. Social skills, risk taking and self esteem
5. Some games our teens play, such as Dungeons and Dragons

It is important to know at least three things to avoid when dealing with a teenager and his or her problems.

Avoid Panic

To react to a crisis with panic is to lessen your chances of gaining a successful solution.

Avoid Pressure

Pressure lures us to a false sense of security. Often the teen gives in to the pressure to do as we ask, only to continue on in avoidance and seclusion.

Avoid Prejudice

Avoid any prejudicing of your interactions with the teen because of the crisis. Don't allow the crisis to cast a dark shadow over your relations with him.

Teens consider suicide, leaving home and loved ones for a variety of reasons, which, to them, are insurmountable:

1. Poor communications with parents
2. Existence or fear of abuse and neglect or sexual exploitation by parents
3. Unreasonable harsh demands or restrictions placed on teens by parents, school, or peers.
4. Problems or disruptions in the family
5. School-related programs

Although there is no single cause of teenage suicide, researchers find certain situations are more likely to trigger underlying emotional problems:

1. Loss of a loved one...a parent, a friend, a boyfriend or girlfriend
2. A major disappointment or humiliation, either real or imagined
3. Lack of communication, especially with parents, about feelings of unhappiness, loneliness, isolation, failure, and frustration
4. Inability to compete in *school, in a job, or society*
5. Lack of a stable family life in a home disrupted by tensions, discord, or alcohol and drug abuse

Is Your Child at Risk?

The teenage years are an emotional roller coaster for parents and children alike. Your teenage child's outlook may swing from elation to despair in a matter of days or even hours. Behavior is often impulsive.

Depression is a major ingredient of teens who take their own lives. A recent study of suicides among young people, has determined that suicidal tendencies are present in one-third of those youths who have mild cases of depression and in three-fourths of those who are severely depressed. (It is also estimated that nearly five percent of all depressed patients actually do die as a result of suicide.)

In a rather shocking case study of suicides among young people, a survey of eighth-grade students in a parochial school, shows that one-third of the children had problems with depression and, indeed, had suicidal thoughts.

What If It Happens to Me?

There are some general tips and hints that should help if you feel that a crisis is at hand.

Implement a cautious, detailed plan of action. It is crucial to cope with your feelings of panic and frustration. There are three vital things that will help you as a family to deal with the problem.

- ADMIT IT! It does no good to take the "Ostrich Approach" and pretend the problem does not exist.
- TALK ABOUT IT! Even if it is painful, it is very important to TALK!
- WRITE ABOUT IT. Involve all family members. This helps to demystify what you are feeling and experiencing at the moment.

Then take positive action:

- Don't lose patience with your child's behavior. It is crucial for you to remain patient even if your teen is expressing some infantile behavior.
- TAKE THREATS SERIOUSLY! Once again, it is crucial to listen to what the child is saying and feeling. Thoughts and threats of suicide often precede the act of suicide.
- Demonstrate your love for the child complete with his hang-ups and problems.
- Don't be afraid to talk to your child about what he is feeling. Tell him or her that all problems can be worked out.
- Once you have established a good base of communication, you can then suggest professional help. Don't be afraid to go with that child to get professional assistance.

What Can We Do to Help?

There are some very important things that pastors, youth ministers, and counselors can do when dealing with a troubled youth.

First, carefully read the combination of "warning" signals that have been previously described.

Be sure to take note whether the individual has suffered a loss or has expressed any other serious problem recently.

It is vital that we not confuse suicidal thoughts with suicidal plans. Over half of our population has had suicidal thoughts, but the thought of suicide does not necessarily mean that the person is a serious risk. Suicide thoughts are far different from the person who knows just what they want to do and how they are going to do it.

It is of major importance that you believe that you can help. Suicidal people may choose to trust a personal friend with their thoughts and feelings, rather than find a professional counselor to confide in.

Further, it is important that you recognize your own feelings. After all, your friend is confiding in you and his or her life may be hanging in the balance. You may be fearful that you will say and do something that may push the youth over the edge. Usually, you are scared because you care. That's okay. Remember, though, your friend is not asking you to be a counselor, he is asking you to listen and to understand. This requires taking a risk and getting involved.

When you have the conviction that the person exhibits all the signs of suicide, what should you do? ASK! Do not feel reluctant to do this. Asking will not make matters worse. In actuality such an inquiry not only yields the information to us, but it also offers relief to the troubled youth. When we are willing to talk about something as uncomfortable as suicide, we prove our willingness to be his friend. It is important to give that person permission to feel what he is feeling. Allowing him to feel these things and to express himself can diminish some of these feelings. Talking about them also lets that person know that in case his feelings get out of control, you are available to talk with him about it.

A number of suicidal intervention programs across the country use a method of assessing the degree of risk. It is called SLAP!

SLAP seeks to find out:

S...Seriousness of intent. Take every cry for help seriously: it's important to discover as quickly as possible how lethal (intent on dying) the person is. Is he/she experiencing so much pain that he/she could easily make a serious attempt at a moments notice?

   Ask these questions:

1. Have you ever thought of killing yourself before?
2. How often do you think about it?
3. Have you ever tried? When? How?
4. Have you thought of how you might do it this time? (It's fair to assume the more detailed the plan, the higher the risk).

103

L...Lethality of method. The method of choice gives some indications as to the level of seriousness or desire to die. Obviously a gun can do far more irreversible damage than a bottle of aspirin. A slit throat is potentially far more serious than a slit wrist. Historically, men have chosen more violent methods than women, but recent reports indicate an increase in violent methods among women. At times the method of choice is simply governed by what is available. There have been kids so intent on dying that they mangled their arms with a plastic picnic knife because it was all they could get.

A...Availability of method. Is the method of choice available? How available is it? The person who is fascinated by ending his or her life with a gun, but doesn't have one, may be at less risk than someone who has decided to use a less violent method but has it available. In deciding the level of risk we must consider both the method of choice and its availability.

P...Proximity to help. The young girl who decides to overdose in an abandoned barn some distance from home or friends should be considered at higher risk than a guy who cuts his wrist in the kitchen when Mom and Dad are in an adjoining room. If a method of choice involves some distance from helping resources (possibility of being discovered), it's of a higher risk.

Although no cry for help should be ignored, **the SLAP** series of questions should give you a more informed sense of the level of seriousness. You're now prepared to make more intelligent decisions on how you should proceed. The young person who has had a fleeting thought of suicide but has gone no further with it presents far less threat than one who has a clearly imagined plan and intention to die.

The high risk person shouldn't be left alone, even for a brief period of time while you summon help.

Caution is needed when it comes to giving philosophical argument. We should search out and help the young person express positive emotions when at all possible. Often the depressed and suicidal individual is not able to use memories of past relationships to bring out positive feelings because he is so intensely focused in on the negative pain he is experiencing now.

Care should be taken not to promise that you can take care of everything. This may be a promise that you won't be able to keep. It may also relieve the individual of the responsibility of any inner control altogether.

After the judgment has been made that the situation is critical, there are some common sense steps to take. This, of course, includes being sure that the means of suicide is not within reach of the individual. For instance, make sure guns, medications, etc. are out of reach.

Tell the person what you plan to do to help. Do not panic or make rash promises, but be calm and firm. Be sure that the communication lines are always open.

Be honest with him about contacting his family or others for help. This involves the person while it makes your intentions clear. We cannot be bound to silence under the guise of confidentiality. Our primary responsibility is to preserve life. I have stated many times, I would rather have someone hate me for 30 years (and live) than feel good about me but act on his/her intentions. If you feel that person is at high risk, get help immediately. Contact a doctor or hospital emergency personnel for help in critical situations.

Chapter 9

How Families Work

The family is God's primary unit for socialization. It was created, not as an afterthought, but as a part of God's original plan. From the beginning, God created the family as a primary institution for the training and development of all human beings. We find this illustrated very clearly in Genesis chapters 2 and 3, where God's intention for family is presented.

A family is not just a collection of individuals, but a system of people who interact with one another. Each individual member, as they interact, impacts the others in a very significant way. There is no greater or more significant relationship developed in human terms than that with the family.

It is also true that the body of Christ is designed to be a family for the people of God. Most of us who were raised within a disfunctional family system, recognize that the best of all parents are far from perfect. We are actualy aware that our needs for significance, acceptance, and approval are not totally met within our family of origin. That is one of the reasons that we need salvation, which comes through belief in the Lord Jesus Christ and His provision for us. We also need the body of Christ. We become members one of another to help and assist each other through the vicissitudes of life.

When families are not functioning well, the balance of the system, the homeostatic balance, can be upset. At times an identified patient can emerge. Many times we see families with teenage children, that one of the teenagers will begin to act out. They may run away, do drugs or alcohol or act out in some other self-destructive or attention seeking manner. Some of this may be caused by peer temptations. Further, the devil attempts to bring about disruption in family life. Many times symptoms of a family that is not functioning well together emerge. It is important to realize that the whole family is in crisis, not just an individual member. Thus, effective intervention requires a willingness to deal with the whole family system.

107

Throughout the rest of this book you will see ways in which we will attempt to impact, not just individuals, but families as well. The goal is to assist them in resolving life's conflicts.

Chapter 10

Financial Crisis

One of the most difficult and stressful areas of marital life is caused by financial mismanagement. There are many questions that a couple needs to ask before marriage. If they are married already, they must come to a place of agreement. Some of the questions include:

1. *Who manages the money?*

   The determination of who manages money is usually determined by who managed it in the family of origin of each individual. In my family, my dad made the money and my mom tried to make it stretch. She was the money manager. That seemed to be functional for my parents, and it was natural for me to assume that my wife would automatically take over that role. As we found, sometimes that works and sometimes it does not. Consideration of various gifts and talents should be allowed for.

2. *What if there is not enough money?*

   Sometimes it is a reality that there is just not enough money coming in to meet the family's financial needs. This can cause tremendous stress on a family. A lack of money can occur for numerous reasons, such as a job loss or significant unemployment caused by a shift in the economy. There are no guarantees that the places we work for will always be there to meet our needs. All embrace the promise that God will meet all our needs according to His glorious riches in Christ Jesus (Philippians 4:19).

Budgeting and understanding God's principles of financial management help. Poor decision making in how to spend money and the use (or misuse) of credit can cause a significant conflict in a relationship. This over burdening of the family with debt can lead to family crisis.

We must learn how to be good stewards of what God allows us to earn. It is important to seek financial counsel. Be sure that you have the proper perspective on the use of money. Jesus taught about the use of money and its priorities. Money in and of itself is not evil, but it is the love (lust) of money that is the root of all evil (1 Timothy 6:10). That is, greed and seeking money as your primary goal in life may lead to long term problems.

We must recognize the need to give generously to the Lord through offerings to the work of God. We should develop a savings plan and an investment strategy that will meet our long term requirements. The advise of John Wesley seems appropriate; make all you can, save all you can, give all you can! All Christians believe that Jesus could come at any time. We may not be around to have to deal with retirement issues, but the reality is that we do not know the day or the time when the Son of Man shall come, therefore we need to plan for the future (Matthew 24:42).

Money Matters: Teens and Children

Many parents have decided not to tell their teens, or children, some of the financial pressures that they are facing. Many young people are shocked when they are faced with the realities of the cost of living. This does not necessarily mean that you should conduct an internal audit with your teens, but, making them aware of bills and general costs of living could very well ease a lot of family arguments that occur today. Many teens go shopping with their parents, but they rarely pay attention to the cost of items. Discussing budget items such as mortgage payments, utilities costs, phone bills, and medical/dental expenses is an eye-opener, and can help prepare teens for adult realities. The financial habits our teens learn now will probably stay with them for life.

A child's or teen's allowance can serve as a training ground in financial matters. Allowances are handled differently by different parents. Some parents make an allowance contingent on work or action. Others provide a child a

110

predetermined sum each week. Other parents pay an allowance on the basis of chores done. However the allowance is determined, giving children spending money helps them learn the value of money, what it will buy, and the cost of things. An allowance that is earned will also teach the value of work, earning money takes time and effort. The intricacies and negotiations of an allowance serve as an excellent training ground and help the teenager appreciate the expenses that are incurred in raising a family.

Jobs for teens can also be a great learning experience. It is crucial to weigh out the pros and cons of a teen having a job. For instance, will the job interfere with school work? If good grades are hard to come by, then perhaps it is not the time to have a job. While scholastic grades and academic records are important, it is also important to understand the psychological needs of the child. For example, it is possible that the added prestige of having a job will help the teen do better academically and scholastically and be an ego builder. On the other hand, will having a job put too much added pressure on the child and make him feel overwhelmed and fearful of failure? It is a very fine line, but it must be faced.

Another ponderous problem, beyond whether or not a child should have the responsibility of a job, is what he or she expects to do with the money earned. Will it go for extra income for the family? Will it be used for his or her education, or put towards that eagerly desired automobile? Or will it go to drugs, video games, or teen parties?

Often teens that feel they have to find a job, will give up their keen interest in sports activities. One young teen who worked through her high school years, expressed some bitterness after graduation because her job prevented her from competing in her favorite sport. These problems should be thoroughly discussed before the decision is finally made. All in all, the majority of teens find their work experiences informative, fun, and profitable. Working teens are able to feel more financially responsible for themselves and display high self- esteem and confidence. The job experience is also beneficial as a form of non-academic education.

Opening savings accounts also helps in setting up budgets and can be helpful to young people, but it is very important to let them make their own decisions when it comes to how that money is used. Obviously, parental guidance is recommended.

Chapter 11

Severe Loss

Divorce

Much like death, divorce creates a huge residual of grief and sorrow for all involved. One of the differences between death and divorce, is that the "corpse" is still walking around.

Statistics indicate that 51.7% of those that married in 1989 were divorced before 1995. This is a telling statistic, indicating the stress that our world has upon married life. A recent survey estimated that in the church the statistics are even worse. Amongst evangelical Christians, a higher number will end up in divorce courts than in non-Christian homes. This is a terrible statistic, and one that we, as the church, need to be aware of and address.

It is important for someone who experiences the crisis of divorce to be able to keep things in perspective. There is usually no completely innocent party in a divorce situation. Divorce is a symptom of a very dysfunctional marriage that, usually, has been perking along in a negative way for a number of years. It is important to recognize that there must be forgiveness, healing and restoration, which can come through the grief process. When forgiveness is exercised, healing comes. The church must teach on the importance of the marital unit and the strength of marriage on a regular basis. We must combat divorce whenever possible. For more teaching on this see my book, *Marriage and Family Life.*

Death and Dying

Because of the importance of these areas of crisis, death and dying are fully addressed in the "Solutions and Treatment" section of this book. Needless to say, death and dying are major life crises, and are of primary concern impacting all of us at some time in our lives.

"The family is the nucleus of civilization."
- William James Durant

"The lack of emotional security of our American young people is due, I believe, to their isolation from the larger family unit. No two people - no mere father and mother - as I have often said, are enough to provide emotional security for a child. He needs to feel himself one in a world of kinfolk, persons of variety in age and temperament, and yet allied to himself by an indissoluble bond which he cannot break if he could, for nature was welded him into it before he was born."
- Pearl S. Buck

SECTION THREE

SOLUTIONS AND TREATMENT

Chapter 12

Solutions to a Crisis Situation

There are several steps that a person can take in order to resolve a crisis. First of all, it is important to recognize that there <u>are</u> solutions to any problem. In order to solve a crisis you must be willing to face it. James 5:16, in many ways, talks about the need to face the truth about a given situation. The concept of a positive confession, that is to deny the reality that you are in a crisis, is not remotely biblical (nor common sense). The truth is, if you are in the crisis of physical illness, you are sick. If you have cancer, that is a tremendous crisis. The reality is, you do have a cancer. To say, "I do not have cancer," would be lying to yourself. You can admit, "I have cancer." At the same time, you can also state, categorically and with great faith, "By His stripes I am healed."

Secondly, in dealing with a crisis, we must help the individual to untangle their projection system. That is, to help them look at things in a more appropriate way. The effect of a crisis on our thinking can be monumental. A crisis can, at least temporarily, reduce our view of the provision of God, His care for us, and minimizes our normal faith to believe God's power to help.

Third, the goal is to assist them in expressing their feelings in an appropriate manner, to speak the truth in love. Thus, it is important that the church create an atmosphere, through pastoral staff and trained leaders, whereby crisis situations can be dealt with in a loving manner, whether developmental or situational.

One of the primary methods of crisis intervention is the Roberts' Seven-State Crisis Intervention Model[6]. The Roberts' Model is an excellent one for longer-term crisis interventions. The stages include:

1. Assessing Lethality

2. Establishing Rapport

119

3. Identifying Major Problems

4. Dealing with Feelings

5. Explore Alternatives

6. Develop an Action Plan

7. Follow-up

Let's look at the usage of this model with a real family counseling situation.

A CASE STUDY

The Richards Family

The Richards family consisting of Mr. Richards, age 37, Mrs. Richards, age 36 and the two Richards' children, Robert, age 15 and Rachel, age 13. Their pastor, James Foresight, referred them to me as he felt their situation was beyond his expertise and in need of immediate intervention.

Plan and Assessment of Lethality

First, their story: Mr. Richards was the initial family spokesperson, interrupted frequently and vociferously by Mrs. Richards. He was very angry about his son's aggressive and "weird" behavior he was exhibiting (as reported by Mrs. Richards) towards his sister and mother. I explored with brief questions the "weird" (sexual overtones towards his sister) and aggression (hitting and threatening), which was episodic and fairly recent. Further, I learned that the son was failing in school and was having difficulty with social (peer) relations. My initial assessment was that though the family was in crisis and transition, it was not in specific danger, and thus safety/lethality issues were minimal.

Developing Rapport

Because of the volatility of the parents, I felt rapport could be best established by seeing each individual separate, for a ½ hour interview, to then bring the family back together for my evaluative presentation. My purpose in this strategic move was two fold. First, to develop personal contact with each family member and affirm their importance in the family. Secondly, I hoped to clarify and understand more fully, from each family member's perspective, their view on the problem. I was especially concerned about the son's reported behavior as viewed by him and other family members, and thus understand mom's over the top need to protect her daughter and punish her son.

Of most importance, I learned from mom that she was extremely concerned about the situation, and wished her husband were more involved. She felt very protective of the daughter and victimized by her son. I then brought the whole family together for my presentation, and to explore the dynamics of the family in greater depth.

Major Problems

The major problems included the following:

- The son and daughter were in normal adolescent transitions, but were not managing it well (developmental crisis).
- The son was not well motivated to study and was disrespectful to mom. Further, he was unclear on boundaries and presented somewhat immature and inappropriate at time.
- Dad was not supportive by presence in the home, due to work schedule and (surmised) interpersonal conflict with Mrs. Richards.
- Mom was clearly enmeshed with her children, and overly anxious regarding seemingly normal dynamics of home life.
- Finally, there seemed to be more to the story, which would only unfold in further investigation.

Provide Support and Deal with Feelings

In the individual sessions and in family counseling I attempted to affirm and support with words and attitude. The overall feelings in the family included mom's anxiety, the son's and daughter's apathy, and the father's frustrations and anger, the later shared somewhat by mom. Supporting the feelings does not mean to agree with their perception, but affirm and care for the person and the family with judgment reserved.

Explore Alternatives

After a time of reflection (so important in counseling, to take time to think about what you are seeing and hearing) I first "described the symptom" of the family, that is, I described the feelings and content of the family narrative from an informed outsider (though concerned). Here is what I saw, which I delicately described.

- The family is in a natural time of transition.
- This is not just the children's problem, but the parent's as well.
- That mom seemed more anxious than needed, though with an expression of genuine concern.
- That the family needed to negotiate this time of transition, and see each other as partners in the process of growth.

The alternative I suggested included:

- For the father to spend more time with his son (especially), taking more responsibility for discipline in the home.
- I recommended continued couple counseling, as I still felt something was unclear in the story of the marriage relationship.
- Develop clear boundaries between the brother and sister and mom, which all agreed to, and which dad could be actively involved in supervising.

Action Plan/Follow-up

The action plan was to implement the three mentioned above, along with seeing the family in 1 month after 3 sessions with mom and dad.

It was during those three sessions that both mom and dad revealed histories of abuse, never previously discussed with each other. Much of mom's anxiety related directly to her daughter's age and maturity level, her husbands seeming lack of interest in mom romantically, along with the fact that two of mom's molesters were her father and her brother. Working through these issues and subsequent problems related to abuse of their past and problems related to adolescent transition and parenting eased the tension and helped stabilize the family.

In this case, with some modification, the Roberts' Model of Crisis Intervention was a most helpful tool. It is best used in organizing the crisis counselor's thinking, especially when working with volatile and fragmented family systems.

Conclusion

The issues addressed in this section are by no means comprehensive. The major crisis issues and transitions have been addressed. In the next section ministry strategies are developed to counteract the problems created by crisis.

ABCD

A model for crisis counseling that is simple and effective is the ABCD model of crisis intervention. Let's look at each point one at a time.

A - ACHIEVE a relationship. To achieve a relationship it is important to listen fully to the individual's problem without judgment, and with great empathy. The listening process shows that you care, and that you are willing to assist the individual in the time of crisis. There is nothing worse than giving trite clichés or pretending to be interested when you really are not. A crisis to you may not be a crisis to someone else. The goal is to first achieve a relationship with the individual who is having the crisis through active listening.

B - BOIL down the problem. Most people, when they are in the middle of a crisis, have a sense that it is astronomical and overwhelming. They often feel hopeless and helpless to resolve the conflict. Part of assisting them is to break down the components of the problem into smaller bites. Boil down the problem so that it can be managed one step at a time.

C - CHALLENGE the individual to take constructive action. Again, looking at things one piece at a time, you assist the person to deal with such questions as, "What can I do now? What can I do tomorrow? What can I do to resolve the problem?" It is very important that the individual in the crisis, with your assistance, develops a positive or constructive action plan to meet the need. If you just give them advice or tell them what to do, you will find, in many cases, your frustration will grow. The average person in crisis has difficulty making decisions. They may say yes to your advise, but take little or no positive action. The frustration comes because you are trying to solve the problem for them, rather than allowing them the dignity of coming up with the solutions for themselves, solutions they are more likely to act upon. We need to allow them opportunity to solve the problem the best that they can, trusting that, with God's help, they will be able to do so.

D - DEVELOP an ongoing plan of action. A one-shot intervention of ministry will not work. There must be a continued relationship and an ongoing plan of action. It is helpful to write these ideas down; develop goals that will make a difference. One hope is to assist the individual to understand how they got to a place where they were vulnerable to this crisis and to be able to learn how to cope more effectively or even avoid this kind of crisis in the future. In order to do so, you must make a commitment to be energetically involved in the lives of those that are in the midst of crisis.

Chapter 13

The Counseling Process

Micro-system Versus Macro-system

In looking at the over-all management of crisis, especially within the family unit, it is important to balance two view points; the micro-system and the macro-system.

Micro-system

Micro-system indicates the actual individual, or small group, counseling process, and techniques that assist people in resolving their conflicts. You deal with the smallest possible unit, the individual in crisis or their family.

We will look at the micro-system issues from a general perspective, as we review the resolution of grief. Much of the process of counseling for individuals is assisting them to face the issues of their lives and work through a standard grief process.

Macro-system

Macro-system speaks to the need for the larger community, including church, to develop services and ministries that will prevent, wherever possible, the crises from occurring or provide for support systems to be able to manage the crises.

The church is in a unique position to provide for the needs of the locality of service. The word of God indicates that the church is the family of God. Within the church we must provide for the needs of those who hurt and are in times of crisis.

Helpful Techniques towards Counseling Resolution

There are several techniques that can assist an individual to resolve crisis issues and problems rooted in their past. One of the goals is to help them face the truth, for knowing the truth will set them free. It is also important to assist them in the process of forgiveness. Forgiveness is a commandment for the believer, highly recommended for all. He said, *"And when you stand praying, if you hold anything against anyone, forgive him, so that your Father in heaven may forgive you your sins"* (Mark 11:25). It is therefore important to process through the anger or hurt caused by crisis, and forgive, and let go of hurts from the past.

There is a three pronged phase of counseling for those who have experienced crisis.

1. *Face It.*

It is important to help the individual face the problem straight ahead. This is usually fairly easy to do since in the midst of crisis one cannot help but see what the crisis is. Part of facing it is taking responsibility in the crisis and obligation to act responsibly toward the crisis. In spite of what has happened, they are responsible to act, believe, and respond in a Christian manner. Pastoral care and counsel should help them to face things directly.

2. *Trace It.*

Trace the origin of the crisis. What things led up to, or precipitated, the crisis. If it is a car accident, there may not have been much you could do to avoid it. It just seemed to happen. That has to be managed, there is nothing to trace. In the case of child abuse, financial mismanagement, divorce, or a death in the family there are usually issues in the person's life that must be walked through. You must trace back to the origins. This is where asking questions and allowing the individual to

126

talk openly and freely is vital and to be encouraged.

3. *Erase It.*

You want to help them say good-bye to the hurts and problems that have been caused. There are several methods by which you can do this.

a) Letter writing or keeping a diary

Assisting someone to write out what they feel and think, in the forms of prayers or letters to those who have hurt them, can help them process through the anger or hurt they may be experiencing. Ultimately, our hope is restoration and reconciliation. In some cases they must go to an individual and make things right. In other cases, this is neither positive nor advisable. Wisdom is required. The letter writing helps them process their feelings in a positive way.

b) *Role playing*

Assisting the individual talk through their hurts is a very helpful technique.

Experiential exercises can help them move past the denial phase and help them in the grief process. A caution must be considered in using techniques, such as using an empty chair to talk to someone who is deceased. Though it may help, depending upon the spiritual maturity of the client, it may be considered as an occult activity. Help them to recognize that if someone from their past, who is no longer living, has hurt them, they must forgive and release. They must accept the forgiveness of the Lord as a part of the process.

Here are some Macro-system services that are very helpful in the management of crisis.

1. *Home Group Ministry*

The small group fellowship, such as a systematic Bible study, prayer meeting, and time of fellowship, helps to meet many needs in the believer's life. People that have a strong social network when a crisis comes are better able to manage it. Those that are connected with a home group are able to manage crisis in a more effective manner. manage it. Those that are connected with a home group are able to manage crisis in a more effective manner.

2. Local Church Counseling Ministry

This may include support groups for assisting those with alcohol and drug abuse problems, adult children of alcoholics, child abuse situations, etc. A professional or pastoral counselor is a strong adjunct to the local church ministry, and trained para-professional counselors can also assist pastoral care.

3. Equipping Ministers

It is an inherent responsibility of the local church to teach and train people to do the work of the ministry (Ephesians 4:11-12). A part of the teaching and training includes:

a) Teaching people parenting skills
b) Marriage and family relationships
c) Financial management
d) Dealing with issues of death and dying, etc.

Seminars and workshops can be brought to the local church to assist with this training. It is a responsibility of the leadership in the locality (local church) to prepare one another for areas of ministry, so that, when crisis times come, we are able to give support and minister effectively.

Assisting to Rebuild Marriages in Times of Crisis

When a crisis occurs within a marital relationship, there are several steps that one can take to assist in the resolution of the crisis.

There are some immediate concerns to be aware of. We must assess the potential for physical violence within the family. When a spouse is in danger of physical abuse, it is strongly recommended that intervention occur. Part of that can include, if necessary, contacting the local police. I don't find anywhere in the word of God, other than persecution for righteousness sake, that indicates we are to accept physical harm. Where physical violence occurs, separation is necessary.

When a crisis occurs in a marriage, as pastoral care people, it is important to seek wisdom from God to know whether to intervene or to wait for them to come and ask for help. Sometimes waiting is the most appropriate response, sometimes direct intervention.

There are certain things that are important to keep in mind in ministering to people in times of crisis, especially when working with couples. They include:

1. *Emotions*

Emotions can run extremely high. Expect the expression of anger, tears, resentment, and bitterness between two people. When emotions run high, judgment is often impaired, and can lead to dangerous acting out.

2. *Time*

All problems take time to develop and all solutions take time to be brought to fruition. Sometimes it has been months or years of silent, sporadic conflict that has finally erupted has finally erupted. What we see in a crisis with a marriage or family is years of problems coming to the surface. Relate the idea that it will take time to find solutions to the people that you are ministering to.

The role of a counselor in this situation is to open lines of communication that are closed when the crisis time comes. Many couples are unable to understand each other. Your role is to act as translator and mediator between the two. This is a Biblical role of adviser, or wise man, as found in the Old Testament. You are to listen to the dispute and attempt to help them to understand and communicate more effectively.

3. *Blame*

People will be focusing the blame on their spouse, rather than focusing on their responsibility in the problem. You must reframe their focus. Look at the crisis, not as the end of a marriage, but as a red flag to help them re-evaluate where they are going with their lives. They must focus on what to do to change the situation. They should ask the question: "What must we do in order to have a stronger marriage?" They must look at themselves for changes.

Some things that are helpful include:

1. Providing an opportunity for a controlled expression of emotions. The expression of feelings is not negative in and of itself. It can cause negative reaction. Allow for the expression of feelings in a controlled manner, without the assassination of character.

2. As a counselor you must remain neutral. Regardless of how injured you feel one party is, and how innocent you feel the other is, it is important to remember that there are no innocent victims with adults. They are both involved in the process of the problem causing and problem solution.

3. Create a forum for them to discuss things openly. Confidentiality and privacy is important.

4. Encourage the couple to talk with each other, not at each other, before God. It is the covenant between each other and before God that keeps marriages together, not the feelings nor the crises.

There are certain things that one should not say in the midst of a marital or family crisis.

1. It is important to recognize that there are no "villains" or "victims." Do not take sides. Although the fault may not always be equal, it takes two to create a marital crisis.

2. Do not assume responsibility for patching up someone's marriage. It is very important that they be responsible for working through the problems in their relationship. None of us, no matter how well trained, are miracle workers when it comes to the self-will of other people. We must not take responsibility for things we are not accountable for.

3. Do not under estimate the potential for acting out, especially of violence, in a domestic quarrel.

4. Be careful of unhealthy attractions, or dependencies, that could form between you and the counselee. Be assured that if you are riding in on your white horse to the rescue, you might be seen as the great savior for their relationship. Harmful affections can develop. Dependencies can be difficult to break. Crisis counseling should be no more than four to six weeks in length. If continuing care is needed, it would be wise to pass that family on to professionally trained counselors who can work through the more significant problems in the marriage.

5. Romans 8:1 says that there is no condemnation to those who are in Christ Jesus. Those with fallen marriages or difficult family situations know about their failures and are often loaded down with guilt and shame. To add insult to injury is not wise. Do not condemn. Try, using the mercy of God, to recognize that but for the grace of God it could be you. Be an encourager, not a judge.

The ministry of crisis counseling is one that must be chosen very carefully. It takes great compassion and patience with wisdom to effectively minister to people who are in times of trouble.

It is important for a local church to recognize that there may be times when people have needs beyond their ability to manage. In such cases, having community resources available is essential. That includes professional counseling services, pastoral care teams, marriage and family counselors, social workers, psychologists, psychiatrists, who have a compatible Christian belief system. Drug and alcohol prevention and treatment programs can be most useful. It is important for the local church to evaluate resources to insure that they are helpful and professional.

Chapter 14

Grief and Loss

The Nature of Grief

"The Lord is nigh unto them that are of a BROKEN HEART *and* SAVETH SUCH *as be of a contrite spirit"* (Psalm 34:18).

Grief is an emotional and physical reaction to a significant personal loss.

No one is immune to grief. Grief comes to everyone and it comes in many different ways. Grief is unique and each of us responds to it in difference ways. Much of our response is based on our incorporated belief system, which is how our parents, church, and other social/cultural setting have taught us to respond. However, there are some common experiences we can draw upon which help us to know about most forms of grief.

1. *Grief Is Painful* - The initial response to grief is that . . . it hurts!

2. *Grief Is Directional* – It has an energy all it's own.

3. *Grief Is Personal* - No one feels grief exactly as you feel it. Your feelings and your circumstances are unique.

4. *Grief Moves Slowly* – It takes time to process through a significant loss.

5. *Grief Includes Mixed Feelings* – The pain and hurt of grief is a most common feeling. Grief may also include other feelings, however, such as guilt and hostility.

6. *Grief Is Natural and Healthy* - Grief is a natural and healthy response to a significant personal loss. There are several reactions that you may experience. They include the following:

133

- TALKING TOO LITTLE

  The client may find it extremely difficult to talk about their deceased loved one or other significant loss.

- REGRESSION

  Under severe stress we tend to regress towards behaviors that give us a sense of warmth and well being.

- TALKING TOO MUCH

  The client may find him/herself talking to their lost loved one, out loud, as though he or she were still present.

- PAINFUL REMINDERS

  The client may feel stabbing grief when they see a reminder of their loved one, such as a photograph, his stamp collection, or a best friend. Further, the client may catch himself/herself talking about the deceased as if he or she were no longer a part of your life.

- GUILT AND SHAME

  The client may love memories involving himself/herself and the person who has died. It is not unusual to feel guilt for being alive, or ashamed of reactions.

- WITHDRAWAL

  Withdrawal, like denial, takes many forms. You may withdraw from the pain of grief, turning to alcohol or other drugs. You may try to escape grief by over activity, such as throwing yourself into your work or joining clubs or groups. You may even temporarily contemplate suicide, the ultimate attempt to withdraw.

- SELF-PITY

  Self-pity is a problem when, months after the death, your consistent conversation starter is something like this: "No one knows how hard life is for me." The self-pity person then proceeds to recite a list of all the bad things that have happened to them. This is futile.

  We can have victory over guilt, shame, bitterness, etc. Because of Jesus' atonement, we can be set free from irrational responses. In order to do so, you can:

  1. Acknowledge your need for forgiveness, either of your "sin," your partner's, or others, and forgive.

  2. Forgive self - first express the negative feelings about yourself.

  3. Accept the Lord's forgiveness according to the Word of God (1 John 1:9).

  4. Resist Satan when he reminds you, or tries to dump the guilt your way.

Grief

I have categorized three primary areas of loss that can occur as people. Those areas are: loss in the area of relationship, loss in the area of events or situations, and loss in the area of self or personal loss such as identity. In each area, a person can deal with these types of losses through the same grief process, which is presented briefly, in the body of this section. For a more comprehensive look at the grief process see my book *Grief Relief.*

Of the many relational losses, the most powerful can be the loss of a beloved animal, friendship, empty nest, the separations of husband and wife, divorce, and a death.

135

a death.

Those people who are unable to say good-bye and work through the problems of loss, who are unable to grieve for the loss of what once was, tend to repeat the same patterns over and over again throughout their life. People carry the problems of the former relationship into the new one.

There can be no greater sense of loss than divorce or death because they are similar and painful. In these cases, the easiest type of loss is perhaps sudden abandonment in divorce, or sudden death. It is the long-term destructive nature of an embittered and battling divorce or a long-term painful illness and death that causes so much of the grief and heartache. In either case, it is important that feelings be shared and that one process through the basic grief cycle presented below.

Types of Loss

Again, there are three primary areas of interpersonal loss. The first are those losses that are age-related as in the loss of a sense of youth or activity level (that is, physical capabilities). The second is occupational loss. The third is the loss of goals or the feeling of loss that is felt when certain things are accomplished or not accomplished.

God has made us as highly complex beings. He said that we are both, *"fearfully and wonderfully made"* (Psalm 139:14a). Yet at the same time our heart is deceitfully wicked. *"Who can understand it"* (Jeremiah 17:9)? When we traverse a time of loss and grief, the grief is experienced in the self or in the soul that God has created. This loss can be devastating to our sense of self-esteem. Loss that leads to grief can leave us in a state of bitterness and despair if not dealt with. This leaves us vulnerable to the works of the enemy and to the works of our own flesh and soul. It is so vital, both as a Christian and as a human being in general, that we learn to deal with the multitude of losses that we are going to experience in a lifetime. The apostle Paul stated that although he had gone through peril, distress, and all kinds of difficulties, he was always more than a conqueror. In spite of all the losses that he experienced, he was able to deal with them and say good-bye, and was able to say *"...Forgetting what is behind and straining toward what is ahead, I press on toward the goal to win the prize for which God has called me heavenward in Christ Jesus"* (Philippians 3:13-14). This is to be our goal. Now let us look to the grief process, and other helpful techniques to assist someone in the throws of a crisis.

The Stages of Grief

There are several stages of grief and mourning; the author's version of these stages are presented here.

Stage One: Shock

The first stage of grief is shock. It is nature's insulation, cushioning the blow. Shock is a physical experience in which you might feel odd physical sensations, a spaced-out feeling, a knot in your stomach, or no appetite.

Stage Two: Denial

Usually the stage after shock is denial. You understand intellectually what has happened, but on a deeper *level,* all of your habits and memories are denying the death or the loss had occurred.

Denial may remain in some form for months or years. There is no set schedule for moving through this stage. Some stay away from the grave or other reminders of their lost loved one, some leave the deceased's room unchanged for a period of time. Do what feels proper for you as you move toward acceptance.

Some forms of denial of death of a loved one are natural, particularly in the early stages of grief. Denial becomes a problem when it is prolonged or extreme.

Denial of death or grief for months and years usually means that the bereaved person is also denying other important aspects of life, such as personal appearances or relationships with others.

137

If this is a problem, talk it over with someone you can trust who will be honest with you. Your pastor or pastoral leadership are good people who can help.

Stage Three: Fantasy Versus Reality

The third stage of your transition is a struggle between fantasy and reality. This can actually be seen as a component of denial.

Stage Four: Grief As a Release

Sooner or later you will come to realize that your loss is real. The pain of this reality penetrates to your deepest self. You cry and weep. Your feelings come pouring out like a fountain of sorrow.

All the normal emotions that have been denied now express themselves; it is a release. Let it flow, let it out! This is one of God's ways of cleansing you from the pain. After this release, much of your physical and emotional pain will fade away. A grieving person who keeps his feelings inside and delays their release for an extended period may experience some reactions.

Stage Five: Learning to Live with Memories

After you have experienced the flood of grief from the previous stage, the pain of grief begins to ease. You are now emerging from the process to the victory.

Learning to live with memories is a longer-term task. You will meet people, go places and see things that remind you of your loss. At this stage, grief is not constant but is aroused by specific incidents.

Stage Six: Acceptance and Affirmation

You are now beginning to accept the loss and to affirm life. Good memories of the deceased are brought to your mind without stabbing pain, and often with gratitude and pleasure for such recollections. You find it easier to talk about your loved one, and to appreciate your past relationship without wishing unrealistically that it could be restored. You show a renewed trust in yourself, as if to say, "I can make it." The process to victory takes years to complete fully. There is no need to hurry it; grief moves at its own pace. Trust the Holy Spirit to do a good work in you.

He who has begun a good work in you will perform it unto the day of Christ Jesus (Philippians 1:6)

You are to find new meaning in what you do. Celebrate the memories of your deceased loved one without being obsessed by the memories. God is love, and His love endures forever. (Psalm 118)

Celebrate the Victory

Death, or other loss, and our response is as much a mystery as it is painful and real. losses of any type leave us with a feeling of bewilderment and frustration. As you grieve, you feel the mystery. You ask, "Why?" and no one seems to have the answer. You hurt, and no one seems able to erase the pain; but through the power of Jesus Christ, we can put death/loss and grief in the context of the Christian faith and hope! This will not automatically clear the mystery, ease the pain, or give you faith and hope, but, in time, the total victory will be yours.

Your hope is found in your relationship with God. He is the source of your hope. God loves you! In your grief, this may not be clear to you. Even Jesus, when He faced death on the cross, cried, *"My God, my God, why hast thou forsaken me?"* (Matthew 27:46). Yet a short time later He said, *"Father, into thy hands I commend my spirit"* (Luke 23:46). Such a victorious step guarantees that there is hope in the face of death and grief. Hope, death, and grief are natural. Hope remains after death and grief are gone. *"Sorrow not, even as others which have no hope"* (1 Thessalonians 4:13).

I only trust that the crises that you will experience, and the critical situations that you will face as a counselor, will be able to be resolved in Christian love and charity. I know for a fact that God loves His people, has a desire to have a relationship with us, gave everything He had, and still gives because He chooses to, for His people. We have a great inheritance. We have a great life. Being a Christian is a trueprivilege, demonstrated as we share our life with others.

APPENDIX 1

The following is taken from Kendah Greenings' book, *7 Tips to Survive a Crisis*, with author's modifications.

1. Face the reality of your loss. Denial is not a way to go.

2. Do something about your problem. Take action. Inaction is fatalism.

3. Avoid the blame syndrome. Don't think the world owes you.

4. Ask for help. To survive you must be practical.

5. Cut your losses. Forgetting those things behind. Hard to do. Give yourself permission to let go.

6. Decide to move on. Don't be crushed if you fail. Job was in crisis; he made it. Many others have. In Christ and with loving support, you can too.

7. Have faith-learn to draw on inner resources of faith (John 5:4). Faith overcomes.

APPENDIX 2

Taken from Elements of Crisis Intervention Greenstone and Leviton, Brooks/Cole Pub. Co. Pacific Grove, CA 1997.

INDICATORS THAT CAN CHARACTERIZE A CRISIS-PRONE PERSON

1. Alienation from lasting and meaningful personal relationships

2. Inability to use life support systems such as family, friends, and social groups

3. Difficulty in learning from experience; the individual continues to make the same mistakes

4. A history of previously experienced crisis that have not been effectively resolved

5. A history of mental disorder or severe emotional imbalance

6. Feelings of low self-esteem

7. Provocative, impulsive behavior resulting from unresolved inner conflict

8. A history of poor marital relationships

9. Excessive use of drugs, including alcohol abuse

10. Marginal income

11. Lack of regular, fulfilling work

12. Unusual or frequent physical injuries

13. Frequent changes in residence

14. Frequent encounters with the law

EVENTS THAT CAN PRECIPITATE A CRISIS

1. An accident in the home

2. An automobile accident, with or without injury

3. Being arrested; appearing in court

4. Changes in job situation and income involving either promotion or demotion

5. Change in school status

6. Death of a significant person in one's life

7. Divorce or separation

8. A delinquency episode either in childhood or adulthood (In childhood: skipping school or running away from home; in adulthood: failure to pay debts)

9. Entry into school

10. Abortion or out-of-wedlock pregnancy

11. Physical illness

12. Acute episodes of mental disorder

13. Retirement

14. Natural disasters

15. Sexual difficulties

16. Major change in living conditions

17. Gaining a new family member (for example, through birth, adoption, or parents or adult children moving in)

18. Dealing with a blended family

19. Foreclosure on a mortgage or loan

20. Actual or impending loss of something significant in one's life

Appendix 3

LIFE CHANGE INDEX SCALE

Look over the events listed in the Life Change Index Scale. Place a check in the space next to a given event if it has happened to you within the last twelve months.

1. Death of spouse	1.	☐	100
2. Divorce	2.	☐	73
3. Marital separation from mate	3.	☐	65
4. Detention in jail or other institution	4.	☐	63
5. Death of a close family member	5.	☐	63
6. Major personal injury or illness	6.	☐	53
7. Marriage	7.	☐	50
8. Being fired at work	8.	☐	47
9. Marital reconciliation	9.	☐	45
10. Retirement from work	10.	☐	45
11. Major change in the health or behavior of a family member	11.	☐	44
12. Pregnancy	12.	☐	40
13. Sexual difficulties	13.	☐	39
14. Gaining a new family member	14.	☐	38
15. Major business readjustment (e.g., merger, reorganization, bankruptcy, etc.)	15.	☐	38
16. Major change in financial state (e.g., either a lot worse off or a lot better off than ususal	16.	☐	37
17. Death of a close friend	17.	☐	36
18. Changing to a different line of work	18.	☐	36
19. Major change in the number of arguments with spouse	19.	☐	35
20. Taking on a mortgage greater than $100, 000 (e.g., purchasing a home, business, etc.)	20.	☐	31
21. Foreclosure ona mortgage or loan	21.	☐	30
22. Major change in responsibilities at work (e.g., promtion, demotion, lateral transfer)	22.	☐	29
23. Son or daugher leaving home (e.g., marriage, attending college,etc.)	23.	☐	29

24. In-law troubles	24.	☐	29
25. Outstanding personal achievement	25.	☐	28
26. Spouse beginnning or ceasing work outside the home	26.	☐	26
27. Beginning or ceasing formal schooling	27.	☐	26
28. Major change in living conditions (e.g., building a new home, remodeling, deterioration of a home or neighborhood)	28.	☐	25
29. Revision of personal habits (dress, manners, associations, etc.)	29.	☐	24
30. Troubles with the boss	30.	☐	23
31. Major change in working hours or conditions	31.	☐	20
32. Change in residence	32.	☐	20
33. Changing to a new school	33.	☐	20
34. Major change in usual type and/or amount of recreation	34.	☐	19
35. Major change in church activities (e.g., a lot more or a lot less than usual)	35.	☐	19
36. Major change in social activities (e.g., clubs, dancing, movies, visiting, etc.)	36.	☐	18
37. Taking on a morgage or loan less than $10,000 (e.g., purchasing a car, TV, freezer, etc.)	37.	☐	17
38. Major change in sleeping habits (a lot more or a lot less sleep or change in time of day when asleep)	38.	☐	16
39. Major change in number of family get-togethers (e.g., a lot more or a lot less than ususal)	39.	☐	15
40. Major change in eating habits (a lot more or a lot less than ususal)	40.	☐	15
41. Vacation	41.	☐	13
42. Christmas	42.	☐	12
43. Minor violations of the law (e.g., traffic tickets, jaywalking, disturbing the peace, etc.)	43.	☐	11

From "The Holmes and Rahe Social Readjustment Rating Scale" by T. Holmes and Rahe in the *Journal of Psychosomatic Research,* 11, 213-218, 1967. Copyright 1967 by Pergamon Press. (Modified slightly by author).

Scoring the Scale

Add the number of points next to each of your check marks. Place the total in the box below.

Total Life Change Units (LCU)

Interpreting Your Score

Dr. Holmes and his colleagues have clearly shown the relationship between recent life changes and future illness. Listed below are the score categories and the associated probability of illness during the next two years for a person with that score.

0-150	No significant problem
150-199	Mild Life Crisis Level with a 35 percent chance of illness
200-299	Moderate Life Crisis Level with a 50 percent chance of illness
300 or over	Major Life Crisis Level with an 80 percent chance of illness

It is not only your life change unit (LCU) total score that is related to your likelihood of illness. Your ability to cope with change has a major effect.

APPENDIX 4

GENERAL REACTIONS OF CHILDREN TO CRISIS

Although many feelings and reactions are shared by people of all ages in response to the direct or indirect effect of crisis, meeting the needs of children requires special attention.

Typical reactions of children, regardless of age, include the following:

- Fears stemming from the crisis extending to their home or neighborhood
- Loss of interest in school
- Regressive behavior
- Sleep disturbances and night terrors
- Fears of events that may be associated with the crisis situation, such as airplane sounds or loud noises.

REACTIONS OF SPECIFIC AGE GROUPS

Children of different age groups tend to react in unique ways to the stress caused by crises and their consequences. The following typical reactions to stress are summarized for each age group and are followed by suggested responses.

Preschool (Ages 1 through 5)

Typical reactions to stress include the following:

- thumb-sucking
- bed-wetting
- fear of the dark or of animals
- clinging to parents
- night terrors
- loss of bladder or bowel control or constipation
- speech difficulties

151

- loss of or increase in appetite
- fear of being left alone
- immobility

Children in this age group are particularly vulnerable to disruption of their previously secure world. Because they lack the verbal and conceptual skills necessary to cope effectively with sudden stress by themselves, they look to family members for comfort. These children are often strongly affected by the reactions of parents and other family members.

Abandonment is a major fear in this age group. Children who have lost family members (or even pets or toys) due to circumstances whether related or unrelated to the crisis will need special reassurance.

The goal of the following responses is to help children integrate their experiences and reestablish a sense of security and mastery:

- Encourage expression through play reenactment where appropriate.
- Provide verbal reassurance and physical comforting.
- Give the child frequent attention.
- Encourage the child's expression of feelings and concerns regarding the loss, temporary or permanent, of family members, pets, toys, or friends.
- Provide comforting bedtime routines.
- Allow the child to sleep in the same room with the parent. Make it clear to the child that this is only for a limited period.

Early Childhood (Ages 5 through 11)

Common reactions to stress in this age group include the following:

- irritability
- whining
- clinging
- aggressive behavior at home or at school
- overt competition with younger siblings for parent's attention

152

- night terrors, nightmares, or fear of darkness
- school avoidance
- loss of interest and poor concentration in school
- fear of personal harm
- confusion
- fear of abandonment
- generalized anxiety

Fear of loss is particularly difficult for these children to handle, and regressive behavior is most typical of this age group.

The following responses may be helpful:

- Patience and tolerance.
- Play sessions with adults and peers where affective reactions can be openly discussed.
- Discussions with adults and peers about frightening, anxiety-producing aspects of events and about appropriate behavior to manage the child's concerns and the stress.
- Relaxation of expectations at school or at home. It should be made clear to the child that this relaxation is temporary and that the normal routine will be resumed after a suitable period.
- Opportunities for structured, but not unusually demanding, chores and responsibilities at home.
- Maintenance of a familiar routine as much a possible and as soon as possible.

Preadolescent (Ages 11 through 14)

The following are common reactions to stress for this age group:

- sleep disturbances
- appetite disturbance
- rebellion in the home
- refusal to do chores

153

- school problems, such as fighting, withdrawal, loss of interest, and attention-seeking behavior
- physical problems, such as headaches, vague aches and pains, skin eruptions, bowel problems, and psychosomatic complaints
- loss of interest in peer social activities
- fear of personal harm
- fear of impeding loss of family members, friends, or home
- anger
- denial
- generalized anxiety

Peer reactions are especially significant in preadolescence. These children need to feel that their fears are both appropriate and shared by others. Responses should be aimed at lessening tensions, anxieties, and possible guilt feelings.

The following responses may be helpful for children in this age group:

- group activities geared toward the resumption of routines
- involvement with same-age group activity
- group discussions geared toward examining feelings about the crisis and appropriate behavior to manage the concerns and the stress
- structured, but undemanding, responsibilities
- temporarily relaxed expectations of performance at school and at home
- additional individual attention and consideration

Adolescent (Age 14 through 18)

Common reactions in this age group include the following:

- psychosomatic symptoms, such as rashes, bowel problems, and asthma
- headaches and tension
- appetite and sleep disturbances
- hypochondriasis
- amenorrhea or dysmenorrhea
- agitation or decrease in energy level

154

- apathy
- decline in interest in the opposite sex
- irresponsible behavior, delinquent behavior, or both
- decline in emancipatory struggles over parental control
- poor concentration
- guilt
- fear of loss

Most of the activities and interests of adolescents are focused in their own age-group peers. Adolescents tend to be especially distressed by the disruption of their peer-group activities and by their lack of access to full adult responsibilities in community efforts.

We recommend the following responses:

- Encourage participation in the community and in individual responses, such as letter writing.
- Encourage discussion of feelings, concerns, and shared information with peers and extrafamily significant others.
- Temporarily reduce expectations for specific levels of both school and general performance, depending on individual reactions.
- Encourage, but do not insist upon, discussions of crisis-induced fears within the family setting.

APPENDIX 7

GUIDELINES FOR EFFECTIVE COMMUNICATIONS IN CRISES

1. **Listen effectively.**
   - Fully hear what the other person is saying.
   - Maintain eye contact if at all possible.
   - Let the other person talk freely.
   - Try to comprehend what the other person is saying.
   - Listen for both feelings and content.
   - Paraphrase the other's statements to gain clarification.
   - Ask for clarification when necessary.
   - Don't let your own feelings get in the way of understanding what the other person is trying to say.

2. **Respond descriptively.**
   - Don't be evaluative in your response; evaluative statements tend to elicit defensiveness.
   - Keep in mind that "rightness" or "wrongness" may not be the issue.
   - Remember, effective communication is not a contest; a "win or lose" mentality is inappropriate.
   - Learn all you can about the other person's thoughts and feelings.
   - Let the other person know some things about you.
   - Use descriptive statements and reveal your reactions to the other person.

3. **Use your own feelings.**
   - Remember that feelings are important in communicating and that they are always present.
   - Practice expressing your feelings.
   - Take responsibility for your feelings.

- Use "I" messages rather than "you" messages; "I" messages reduce threat to the other person.
- Use descriptive statements that contain feelings.
- Be clear and specific about your feelings.

4. Assess needs.
- Consider the needs of all involved.
- Address issues over which the victim has actual control.
- Avoid being judgmental and critical; avoid preaching.

5. Make timely responses.
- Deliver responses at the time they are most important.
- Deliver responses as soon as possible after the behavior that requires response.
- Do not store up old concerns for later discussion.
- Do not use old or saved concerns as a weapon.
- Assess whether the other person is ready to handle your responses at this time.
- Consider delaying responses on sensitive issues until you are in a more appropriate setting.
- Discuss emotional issues in private.
- Practice communication skills for greatest effectiveness.

LISTENING

During conversations with victims, keep in mind the following items about the imporance of listening:

1. Listening is basic to successful communications.
2. Listening requires responsiveness.
3. Listening enables the listener to know more about the speaker.
4. Listening encourages expression.
5. Listening allows exploration of both feelings and content.
6. Listening helps establish trust between the parties.
7. Listening allows greater accuracy of communication.

8. Listening requires practice and is not always easy to learn.
9. Listening includes listening for content, feelings, and point of view.
10. Listening lets the speaker relax.
11. Attitudes and feelings may be conveyed nonverbally.

When you listen, remember to do the following:

1. Attend to verbal content.
2. Attend to nonverbal cues.
3. Hear and observe.
4. Attend to the feelings expressed by the speaker.
5. Don't think about other things when you are listening to someone.
6. Don't listen with only "half an ear".
7. Become attuned to the speaker's verbal and nonverbal messages.
8. Note any extra emphasis the speaker places on certain words.
9. Notice the speaker's speech patterns and recurring themes.

NONVERBAL COMMUNICATIONS

The following are examples of nonverbal acts a speaker may use to communiciate:

- Sighing
- Flipping through papers
- Wincing
- Looking around, up, or down
- Smoking
- Chewing gum
- Yawning
- Tapping a finger or foot
- Frowning
- Displaying nervousness
- Avoiding eye contact
- Saying nothing
- Making jerky gestures
- Dressing sloppily
- Blinking rapidly

- Constantly looking at a clock or watch
- Showing favoritism
- Acting bored
- Being drunk

Certain nonverbal cues can indicate a specific attitude. Some examples follow:

Nonverbal Cues that May Indicate Openness

- Uncrossed legs
- Open hands
- Unbuttoned coat, or unbuttoning the coat
- Hands spread apart
- Palms up
- Leaning forward

Nonverbal Cues that May Indicate Defensiveness

- Fists closed
- Arms crossed in front of individual
- Legs crossed
- One leg over the chair arm

Nonverbal Cues that May Indicate Cooperation

- Opening coat
- Tilted head
- Sitting on the edge of a chair
- Eye contact
- Hand-to-face gestures
- Leaning forward

Nonverbal Cues that May Indicate Evaluating

- Head tilted
- Chin stroking
- Looking over glasses
- Pacing
- Pinching the bridge of the nose

Nonverbal Cues that May Indicate Readiness

- Hands on hips
- Leaning forward
- Confident speech
- Moving closer to the other person

Nonverbal Cues that May Indicate Suspicion

- Lack of eye contact
- Glancing sideways at the other person
- Body apparently pointed toward exit from area
- Touching the bridge of the nose
- Rubbing the ears
- Rubbing the eyes

Nonverbal Cues that May Indicate Confidence

- Elevating oneself by sitting on a higher chair or standing on a platform
- Finger "steepling"
- Hands clasped behind the back
- Feet on a desk or table
- Leaning on an object
- Clucking sound
- Leaning back, with both hands supporting the neck

APPENDIX 6

SCRIPTURES RELATED TO CRISIS

ABUSE

Psalm 34:4,5
I sought the Lord, and He answered me, And delivered me from all my fears. The looked to Him and were radiant, And their faces shall never be ashamed.

1 Peter 5:7
casting all your anxiety upon Him, because He cares for you.

Psalm 42:11
Why are you in despair, O my soul? And why have you become disturbed within me? Hope in God, for I shall yet praise Him, The help of my countenance, and my God.

ADULTERY

Proverbs 6:32
The one who commits adultery with a woman is lacking sense; He who would destroy himself does it.

Matthew 5:27,28
"You have heard that it was said, 'You shall not commit adultery'; but I say to you, that everyone who looks on a woman to lust for her has committed adultery with her already in his heart."

Luke 16:18
"Everyone who divorces his wife and marries another commits adultery; and he who marries one who is divorced from a husband commits adultery."

Matthew 15:19

"For out of the heart come evil thoughts, murders, adulteries, fornications, thefts, false witness, slanders."

Proverbs 28:13

He who conceals his transgressions will not prosper. But he who confesses and forsakes *them* will find compassion.

1 John 1:9

If we confess our sins, He is faithful and righteous to forgive us our sins and to cleanse us from all unrighteousness.

ALCOHOL

Proverbs 20:1

Wine is a mocker, strong drink a brawler, And whoever is intoxicated by it is not wise.

Proverbs 23:20, 21

Do not be with heavy drinkers of wine, *Or* with gluttonous eaters of meat;

1 Corinthians 6:9,10

Or do you not know that the unrighteous shall not inherit the kingdom of God? Do not be deceived; neither fornicators, nor idolaters, nor adulterers, nor effeminate, nor homosexuals, nor thieves, nor *the* covetous, nor drunkards, nor revilers, nor swindlers, shall inherit the kingdom of God.

Ephesians 5:18

And do not get drunk with wine, for that is dissipation, but be filled with the Spirit,

ANGER

Proverbs 29:11

A fool always loses his temper, But a wise man holds it back.

Matthew 5:21, 22

"You have heard that the ancients were told, 'You shall not commit murder' and 'Whoever commits murder shall be liable to the court.' But I say to you that everyone who is angry with his brother shall be guilty before the court; and whoever shall say to his brother, 'Raca,'" shall be guilty before the supreme court; and whoever shall say, "You fool,' shall be guilty *enough to go* into the fiery hell."

ANXIETY

Proverbs 3:5,6

Trust in the Lord with all your heart, And do not lean on your own understanding. In all your ways acknowledge Him, And He will make your paths straight.

Psalm 42:11

Why are you in despair, O my soul? And why have you become disturbed within me? Hope in God, for I shall yet praise Him, The help of my countenance, and my God.

Psalm 34:4

I sought the Lord, and He answered me, And delivered me from all my fears.

Psalm 55:22

Cast your burden upon the Lord, and He will sustain you; He will never allow the righteous to be shaken.

Philippians 4:6,7

Be anxious for nothing, but in everything by prayer and supplication with thanksgiving let your requests be made known to God. And the peace of God, which surpasses all comprehension, shall guard you hearts and your minds in Christ Jesus.

Romans 8:28

And we know that God causes all things to work together for good to those who love God, to those who are called according to *His* purpose.

ATTITUDE

Ephesians 4:22-24
that, in reference to your former manner of life, you lay aside the old self, which is being corrupted in accordance with the lusts of deceit, and that you be renewed in the spirit of your mind, and put on the new self, which in *the likeness of* God has been created in righteousness and holiness of the truth.

Colossians 3:15
And let the peace of Christ rule in your hearts, to which indeed you were called in one body; and be thankful.

BAD HABITS

Psalm 119:11
Thy word I have treasured in my heart, That I may not sin against Thee.

James 4:7
Submit therefore to God. Resist the devil and he will flee from you.

BEAUTY

Philippians 4:8
Finally, brethren, whatever is true, whatever is honorable, whatever is right, whatever is pure, whatever is lovely, whatever is of good repute, if there is any excellence and if anything worthy of praise, let your mind dwell on these things.

BITTERNESS

Ephesians 4:31, 32
Let all bitterness and wrath and anger and clamor and slander be put away from you, along with all malice. Be kind to one another, tender-hearted, forgiving each other, just as God in Christ also has forgiven you.

Hebrews 12:14, 15
Pursue peace with all men and the sanctification without which no one will se the Lord. See to it that no one comes short of the grace of God; that no root of bitterness springing up causes trouble, and by it many be defiled.

BORN AGAIN

John 3:16
For God so loved the world, that He gave His only begotten Son, that whoever believes in Him shall not perish, but have eternal life.

John 1:12, 13
But as many as received Him, to them He gave the right to become children of God, even to those who believe in His name, who were born, not of blood nor of the will of the flesh nor of the will of man, but of God.

Romans 8:1
There is therefore now no condemnation for those who are in Christ Jesus.

CHURCH

2 Timothy 2:19
Nevertheless, the firm foundation of God stands, having this seal, "The Lord knows those who are His," and, "Let everyone who names the name of the Lord abstain from wickedness."

1 Peter 2: 5,9
You also, as living stones, are being built up as a spiritual house for a holy priesthood, to offer up spiritual sacrifices acceptable to God through Jesus Christ. But you are a chosen race, a royal priesthood, a holy nation, a people for God's own possession, that you may proclaim the excellencies of Him who has called your out of darkness into His marvelous light;

Hebrews 10:25
Not forsaking our own assembling together, as is the habit of some, but encouraging *one another;* and all the more, as you see the day drawing near.

COMPASSION

Colossians 3:12
And so, as those who have been chosen of God, holy and beloved, put on a heart of compassion, kindness, humility, gentleness and patience;

James 1:27
This is pure and undefiled religion in the sight of *our* God and Father, to visit orphans and widows in their distress, *and* to keep oneself unstained by the world.

CONCEIT

Proverbs 16:18,19
Pride *goes* before destruction, And a haughty spirit before stumbling. It is better to be of a humble spirit with the lowly, Than to divide the spoil with the proud.

CONFESSION

Psalm 32:5
I acknowledged my sin to Thee, And my iniquity I did not hide; I said, "I will confess my transgressions to the Lord"; And Thou didst forgive the guilt of my sin.

1 John 1:9
If we confess our sins, He is faithful and righteous to forgive us our sins and to cleanse us from all unrighteousness.

James 5:16
Therefore, confess your sins to one another, and pray for one another, so that you may be healed. The effective prayer of a righteous man can accomplish much.

CONFIDENCE

Proverbs 3:26
For the Lord will be your confidence, And will keep your foot from being caught.

Psalm 118:8,9
It is better to take refuge in the Lord Than to trust in man. It is better to take refuge in the Lord Than to trust in princes.

Psalm 71:5
For Thou are my hope; O Lord God, *Thou are* my confidence form my youth.

Proverbs 14:26
In the fear of the Lord there is strong confidence, And his children will have refuge.

1 John 3:21
Beloved, if our heart does not condemn us, we have confidence before God;

1 John 5:14,15
And this is the confidence which we have before Him, that, if we ask anything according to His will, He hears us.

CONFORMITY

Romans 12:1,2
I urge you therefore, brethren, by the mercies of God, to present our bodies a living and holy sacrifice, acceptable to God, *which is* your spiritual service of worship. And do not be conformed to this world, but be transformed by the renewing of your mind, that you may prove what the will of God is, that which is good and acceptable and perfect.

2 Corinthians 6:14,17,18

Do not be bound together with unbelievers; for what partnership have righteousness and lawlessness, or what fellowship has light with darkness? "Therefore, come out from their midst and be separate," says the Lord. "And do not touch what is unclean; And I will welcome you. And I will be a father to you. And you shall be sons and daughters to Me," Says the Lord Almighty.

COURAGE

Deuteronomy 31:6

"Be strong and courageous, do not be afraid or tremble at them, for the Lord you God is the one who goes with you. He will not fail your or forsake you."

DEATH

Psalm 116:15

Precious in the sight of the Lord Is the death of His godly ones.

Psalm 23:4

Even though I walk through the valley of the shadow of death, I fear no evil; for Thou art with me; Thy rod and Thy staff, they comfort me.

Romans 6:23

For the wages of sin is death, but the free gift of God is eternal life in Christ Jesus our Lord.

John 11:25,26

Jesus said to her, "I am the resurrection and the life; he who believes in Me shall live even if he dies, and everyone who lives and believes in Me shall never die. Do you believe this?"

Hebrews 9:27,28
And inasmuch as it is appointed for men to die once and after this *comes* judgment, so Christ also, having been offered once to bear the sins of many, shall appear a second time for salvation without *reference to* sin, to those who eagerly await Him.

1 Thessalonians 4:14
For if believe that Jesus died and rose again, even so God will bring with Him those who have fallen asleep in Jesus.

1 John 3:2
Beloved, now we are children of God, and it has not appeared as yet what we shall be. We know that, when he appears, we shall be like Him, because we shall see Him just as He is.

Revelation 21:4
and He shall wipe away every tear from their eyes; and there shall no longer be *any* death; there shall no longer be *any* mourning, or crying, or pain; the first things have passed away."

1 Corinthians 15:55-57
"O death, where is your victory? O death, where is your sting?" The sting of death is sin, and the power of sin is the law; but thanks be to God, who gives us the victory through our Lord Jesus Christ.

Leviticus 19:11
'You shall not steal, nor deal falsely, nor lie to one another.'

DEFEAT

Proverbs 24:16
For a righteous man falls seven times, and rises again, But the wicked stumble in *time of* calamity.

2 Corinthians 4:16
Therefore we do not lose heart, but though our outer man is decaying, yet our inner man is being renewed day by day.

2 Corinthians 12:9
And He has said to me, "My grace is sufficient for you, for power is perfected in weakness." Most gladly, therefore, I will rather boast about my weaknesses, that the power of Christ may dwell in me.

DEMONS

James 4:7
Submit therefore to God. Resist the devil and he will flee from you.

DEPRESSION

1 John 4:4
You are from God, little children, and have overcome them; because greater is He who is in you than he who is in the world.

Psalm 42:11
Why are you in despair, O my soul? And why have you become disturbed within me? Hope in God, for I shall yet praise Him, The help of my countenance, and my God.

Isaiah 26:3
"The steadfast of mind Thou wilt keep in perfect peace, Because he trusts in Thee."

Isaiah 40:29
He gives strength to the weary, And to *him who* lacks might He increases power.

Isaiah 53:4,5
Surely our grief's He Himself bore, And our sorrows He carried; Yet we ourselves esteemed Him stricken, Smitten of God, and afflicted. But He was pierced through for our transgressions, He was crushed for our iniquities; The chastening for our well-being *fell* upon Him, And by His scourging we are healed.

Nehemiah 8:10
Then he said to them, "Go, eat of the fat, drink of the sweet, and send portions to him who had nothing prepared; for this day is holy to our Lord. Do not be grieved, for the joy of the Lord is you strength."

John 14:27
"Peace I leave with you; My peace I give to you; not as the world gives, do I give to you. Let not your heart be troubled, nor let it be fearful."

DISCOURAGEMENT

Psalm 147:3
He heals the brokenhearted and binds up their wounds.

2 Corinthians 4:8, 14
We are afflicted in every way, but not crushed; perplexed, but not despairing…knowing that He who raised the Lord Jesus will raise us also with Jesus and will present us with you.

Proverbs 17:22
A joyful heart is good medicine, But a broken spirit dries up the bones.

Psalm 51:17
The sacrifices of God are a broken spirit; A broken and a contrite heart, O God, You will not despise.

DIVORCE

Genesis 2:24
For this reason a man shall leave his father and his mother, and be joined to his wife; and they shall become one flesh.

Matthew 5:31, 32
It was said, Whoever sends his wife away, let him give her a certificate of divorce; but I say to you that everyone who divorces his wife, except for the reason of unchastity, makes her commit adultery; and whoever marries a divorced woman commits adultery.

Mark 10:11, 12
And He said to them, Whoever divorces his wife and marries another woman commits adultery against her; and if she herself divorces her husband and marries another man, she is committing adultery.

1 Corinthians 7:10, 11
But to the married I give instructions, not I, but the Lord, that the wife should not leave her husband (but if she does leave, she must remain unmarried, or else be reconciled to her husband), and that the husband should not divorce his wife.

DOUBT

Hebrews 11:6
And without faith it is impossible to please Him, for he who comes to God must believe that He is and that He is a rewarder of those who seek Him.

James 1:5-7
But if any of you lacks wisdom, let him ask of God, who gives to all generously and without reproach, and it will be given to him. But he must ask in faith without any doubting, for the one who doubts is like the surf of the sea, driven and tossed by the wind. For that man ought not to expect that he will receive anything from the Lord.

Hebrews 12:1, 2
Therefore, since we have so great a cloud of witnesses surrounding us, let us also lay aside every encumbrance and the sin which so easily entangles us, and let us run with endurance the race that is set before us, fixing our eyes on Jesus, the author and perfecter of faith, who for the joy set before Him endured the cross, despising the shame, and has sat down at the right hand of the throne of God.

DRUG ABUSE

2 Timothy 1:7
For God has not given us a spirit of timidity, but of power and love and discipline.

James 1:14, 15
But each one is tempted when he is carried away and enticed by his own lust. Then when lust has conceived, it gives birth to sin; and when sin is accomplished, it brings forth death.

ENEMIES

Romans 12:17-19
Never pay back evil for evil to anyone. Respect what is right in the sight of all men. If possible, so far as it depends on you, be at peace with all men. Never take you own revenge beloved, but leave room for the wrath of God, for it is written, "Vengeance is Mine, I will repay," says the Lord.

Matthew 5:43, 44
You have heard that it was said, "You shall love your neighbor and hat your enemy. But I say to you, love your enemies and pray for those who persecute you."

Matthew 18:21, 22
Then Peter came and said to Him, "Lord, how often shall my brother sin against me and I forgive him? Up to seven times?" Jesus said to him, "I do not say to you, up tot seven times, but up to seventy times seven."

175

Psalm 97:10
Hate evil, you who love the Lord, who preserves the souls of His godly ones; He delivers them from the hand of the wicked.

FAITH

Hebrews 11:1
Now faith is the assurance of things hoped for, the conviction of things not seen.

Hebrews 11:6
And without faith it is impossible to please Him, for he who comes to God must believe that He is and that He is a rewarder of those who seek Him.

Romans 10:17
So faith comes from hearing, and hearing by the word of Christ.

Ephesians 2:8, 9
For by grace you have been saved through faith; and not of yourselves, it is the gift of God; not as a result of works, so that no one may boast.

Romans 14:23
But he who doubts is condemned if he eats, because his eating is not from faith, and whatever is not from faith is sin.

FEAR

Psalm 34:4
I sought the Lord, and He answered me, and delivered me from all my fears.

John 14:27
Peace I leave with you; My peace I give to you; not as the world gives do I give to you. Do not let your heart be troubled, nor let it be fearful.

Isaiah 41:10
Do not fear, for I am with you; do not anxiously look about you, for I am your
God. I will strengthen you, surely I will help you, surely I will uphold you with My
righteous right hand.

Philippians 4:6, 7
Be anxious for nothing, but in everything by prayer and supplication with thanksgiving
let your requests be made known to God.

Hebrews 13:5, 6
Make sure that your character is free from the love of money, being content with
what you have; for He Himself has said, "I will never desert you, nor will I ever
forsake you," so that we confidently say, "The Lord is my helper, I will not be
afraid, what will man do to me?"

FORGIVENESS

Psalm 32:1, 2
How blessed is he whose transgression is forgiven, whose sin is covered! How
blessed is the man to whom the Lord does not impute iniquity, and in whose spirit
there is no deceit!

Psalm 51:1, 2
Be gracious to me, O God, according to Your lovingkindness; according to the
greatness of Your compassion blot out my transgressions. Wash me thoroughly
from my iniquity and cleanse me from my sin.

Isaiah 43:25
I, even I, am the one who wipes out your transgressions for My own sake, and I
will not remember your sins.

Psalm 103:2-5

Bless the Lord, O my soul, and forget none of His benefits; who pardons all your iniquities, who heals all your diseases; who redeems your life from the pit, who crowns you with lovingkindness and compassion; who satisfies your years with good things, so that your youth is renewed like the eagle.

Matthew 5:7

Blessed are the merciful, for they shall receive mercy.

Mark 11:25, 26

Whenever you stand praying forgive, if you have anything against anyone, so that your Father who is in heaven will also forgive you your transgressions. But if you do not forgive, neither will your Father who is in heaven forgive your transgressions.

Proverbs 25:21, 22

If your enemy is hungry, give him food to eat; and if he is thirsty, give him water to drink. For you will heap burning coals on his head, and the Lord will reward you.

Ephesians 4:32

Be kind to one another, tender-hearted, forgiving each other, just as God in Christ also has forgiven you.

FRIENDS

Proverbs 17:17

A friend loves as all times, and a brother is born for adversity.

Amos 3:3

Do two men walk together unless they have made an appointment?

Galatians 6:2

Bear one another's burdens, and thereby fulfill the law of Christ.

Proverbs 27:6

Faithful are the wounds of a friend, but deceitful are the kisses of an enemy.

Proverbs 17:9
He who conceals a transgression seeks love, But he who repeats a matter separates intimate friends.

Ecclesiastes 4:10
For if either of them falls, the one will lift up his companion. But woe to the one who falls when there is not another to lift him up.

Romans 12:15
Rejoice with those who rejoice, and weep with those who weep.

Proverbs 13:20
He who walks with wise men will be wise, but the companion of fools will suffer harm.

Proverbs 27:10
Do not forsake your own friend or your father's friend, and do not go to your brother's house in the day of your calamity; better is a neighbor who is near than a brother far away.

FUTURE

Proverbs 3:1, 2
My son, do not forget my teaching, but let your heart keep my commandments; for length of days and years of life and peace they will add to you.

1 John 2:17
The world is passing away, and also its lusts; by the one who does the will of God lives forever.

Proverbs 16:9
The mind of man plans his way, but the Lord directs his steps.

Proverbs 16:3
Commit your works to the Lord and your plans will be established.

Mark 9:23
And Jesus said to him, "If You can? All things are possible to him who believes."

Proverbs 15:22
Without consultation, plans are frustrated, but with many counselors they succeed.

Jeremiah 29:11
For I know the plans that I have for you, declares the Lord, plans for welfare and not for calamity to give you a future and a hope.

John 14:2, 3
In My Father's house are many dwelling places; if it were not so, I would have told you; for I go to prepare a place for you. If I go and prepare a place for you, I will come again and receive you to Myself, that where I am, there you may be also.

GIFTS FROM GOD

Romans 6:23
For the wages of sin is death, but the free gift of God is eternal life in Christ Jesus our Lord.

GIVING

Proverbs 21:26
All day long he is craving, while the righteous gives and does not hold back.

Matthew 10:8
…Freely you received, freely give.

Matthew 10:42
And whoever in the name of disciple gives to one of these little ones even a cup of cold water to drink, truly I say to you, he shall not lose his reward.

Proverbs 11:25
The generous man will be prosperous, and he who waters will himself be watered.

GOALS

Psalm 37:4, 5
Delight yourself in the Lord; and He will give you the desires of your heart. Commit your way to the Lord, trust also in Him, and He will do it.

1 Corinthians 9:24, 25
Do you not know that those who run in a race all run, but only one receives the prize? Run in such a way that you may win. Everyone who competes in the games exercises self-control in all things. They then do it to receive a perishable wreath, but we an imperishable.

Galatians 6:9
Let us not lose heart in doing good, for in due time we will reap if we do not grow weary.

GRIEF

Matthew 5:4
Blessed are those who mourn, for they shall be comforted.

John 11:35, 36
Jesus wept. So the Jews were saying, "See how He loved him!"

John 14:1
"Believe Me that I am in the Father and the Father is in Me; otherwise believe because of the works themselves."

1 Peter 1:3-5
Blessed be the God and Father of our Lord Jesus Christ, who according to His great mercy has caused us to be born again to a living hope through the resurrection of Jesus Christ from the dead, to obtain an inheritance which is imperishable and

undefiled and will not fade away, reserved in heaven for you, who are protected by the power of God through faith for a salvation ready to be revealed in the last time.

1 Thessalonians 4:13, 14
But we do not want you to be uninformed, brethren, about those who are asleep, so that you will not grieve as do the rest who have no hope. For if we believe that Jesus died and rose again, even so God will bring with Him those who have fallen asleep in Jesus.

GUILT

Psalm 32:3, 5
When I kept silent about my sin, my body wasted away through my groaning all day long. I acknowledged my sin to You, and my iniquity I did not hide; I said, "I will confess my transgressions to the Lord"; And You forgave the guild of my sin.

Psalm 103:12
As far as the east if from the west, so fare has He removed our transgressions from us.

2 Chronicles 30:9
For the Lord your God is gracious and compassionate, and will not turn His face away from you if you return to Him.

HEALING

James 5:13-16
Is anyone among you suffering? Then he must pray. Is anyone cheerful? He is to sing praises. Is anyone among you sick? The he must call for the elders of the church and they are to pray over him, anointing him with oil in the name of the Lord; and the prayer offered in faith will restore the one who is sick, and the Lord will raise him up, and if he has committed sins, they will be forgiven him. Therefore, confess your sins to one another, and pray for one another so that you may be healed. The effective prayer of a righteous man can accomplish much.

Isaiah 40:29, 31
He gives strength to the weary, and to him who lacks might he increases power.
Yet those who wait for the Lord will gain new strength; they will mount up with
wings like eagles, they will run and not get tired, they will walk and not become
weary.

Jeremiah 30:17
For I will restore you to health and I will heal you of your wounds, declares the
Lord, Because they have called you an outcast, saying: it is Zion; no one cares for
her."

Psalm 103:1
Bless the Lord, O my soul, And all that is within me, bless His holy name. Who
pardons all your iniquities, who heals all your diseases.

Psalm 147:3
He heals the broken hearted and bind up their wounds.

1 Peter 2:24
And He himself bore our sins in His body on the cross, so that we might die to sin
and live to righteousness; for by His wounds we are healed.

HEAVEN

1 John 3:2
And He Himself is the propitiation for our sins; and not for ours only, but also for
those of the whole world.

1 Corinthians 15:51, 52
Behold, I tell you a mystery; we will not all sleep, but we will all be changed, in a
moment, in the twinkling of an eye, at the last trumpet; for the trumpet will sound,
and the dead will be raised imperishable, and we will be changed.

HOME

Joshua 24:15
....Choose for yourselves today whom you will serve; but as for me and my house, we will serve the Lord.

HONESTY

Luke 8:11, 15
Now the parable is this: the seed is the word of God. But the see in the good soil, these are the ones who have heard the word in an honest and good heart, and hold it fast, and bear fruit with perseverance.

Psalm 24:3, 4
Indeed, none of those who wait for you will be ashamed; those who deal treacherously without cause will be ashamed. Make me know Your ways, O Lord; teach me Your paths.

Proverbs 16:8
Better is a little with righteousness than great income with injustice.

HUMILITY

Philippians 2:5-8
Have this attitude in yourselves which was also in Christ Jesus, who, although He existed in the form of God, did not regard equality with God a thing to be grasped, but emptied Himself, taking the form of a bond-servant, and being made in the likeness of men. Being found in appearance as a man, He humbled Himself by becoming obedient to the point of death on the cross.

2 Chronicles 7:14
And My people who are called by My name humble themselves and pray and seek My face and turn from their wicked ways, then I will hear from heaven, will forgive their sin and will heal their land.

Proverbs 15:33
The fear of the Lord is instruction fro wisdom, and before honor comes humility.

Matthew 18:4
Whoever then humbles himself as this child, he is the greatest in the kingdom of heaven.

James 4:6
God is opposed to the proud, but gives grace to the humble.

1 Peter 5:6
Therefore humble yourselves under the mighty hand of God, that He may exalt you at the proper time.

INCEST

Leviticus 18:6, 7
None of you shall approach any blood relative of his to uncover nakedness; I am the Lord. You shall not uncover the nakedness of your father, that is, the nakedness of your mother. She is your mother; you are not to uncover her nakedness.

Leviticus 18:29
For whoever does any of these abominations, those persons who do so shall be cut off from among their people.

Psalm 27:10
For my father and my mother have forsaken me, but the Lord will take my up.

Isaiah 41:10, 11, 13
Do not fear, for I am with you; do not anxiously took about you, for I am your God. I will strengthen you, surely I will help you, surely I will uphold you with My righteous right hand. Behold, all those who are angered at you will be shamed and dishonored; those who contend with you will be as nothing and will perish. For I am the Lord your God, who upholds your right hand, who says to you, do not fear, I will help you.

LONELINESS

Psalm 68:5
A father of the fatherless and a judge for the widows, Is God in His holy habitation.

Psalm 46:1-3
God is our refuge and strength, A very present help in trouble. Therefore we will not fear, though the earth should change And though the mountains slip into the heart of the sea; Though its water roar *and* foam, Though the mountains quake at its swelling pride.

Genesis 28:15
"Behold, I am with you and will keep you wherever you go, and will bring you back to this land; for I will not leave you until I have done what I have promised you."

John 14:18
"I will not leave you as orphans; I will come to you."

Hebrews 13:5,6
Make sure that your character is free from the love of money, being content with what you have; for He Himself has said, "I will never desert you, nor will I ever forsake you," so that we confidently say, "The Lord is my helper, I will not be afraid. What will man do to me?"

Matthew 28:20
"teaching them to observe all that I commanded you; and lo, I am with you always, even to the end of the age."

LOVE

1 John 4:10
In this is love, not that we loved God, but that He loved us and sent His Son *to be* the propitiation for our sins.

John 3:16
"For God so loved the world, that He gave His only begotten Son, that whoever believes in Him shall not perish, but have eternal life."

1 John 3:1
See how great a love the Father has bestowed on us, that we would be called children of God; and *such* we are. For this reason the world does not know us, because it did not know Him.

Romans 12:9,10
Let love *be* without hypocrisy. Abhor what is evil; cling to what is good. *Be* devoted to one another in brotherly love; give preference to one another in honor;

John 13:34,35
"A new commandment I give to you, that you love one another, even as I have loved you, that you also love one another. By this all men will know that you are My disciples, if you have love for one another."

1 Corinthians 13:4-8
Love is patient, love is kind *and* is not jealous; love does not brag *and* is not arrogant, does not act unbecomingly; it does not seek its own, is not provoked, does not take into account a wrong *suffered*, does not rejoice in unrighteousness, but rejoices with the truth; bears all things, believes all things, hopes all things, endures all things. Love never fails; but if *there are gifts of* prophecy, they will be done away; if *there are* tongues, they will cease; if *there is* knowledge, it will be done away.

MARRIAGE

Genesis 2:18, 23, 24
Then the Lord God said, "It is not good for the man to be alone; I will make him a helper suitable for him." The man said, "This is now bone of my bones, And flesh of my flesh; She shall be called Woman, Because she was taken out of Man." For this reason a man shall leave his father and his mother, and be joined to his wife; and they shall become one flesh.

Proverbs 18:22
He who finds a wife finds a good thing And obtains favor from the Lord.

2 Corinthians 6:14
Do not be bound together with unbelievers; for what partnership have righteousness and lawlessness, or what fellowship has light with darkness?

Ephesians 5:21,22
and be subject to one another in the fear of Christ. Wives, *be subject* to your own husbands, as to the Lord.

1 Peter 3:7
You husbands in the same way, live with *your wives* in an understanding way, as with someone weaker, since she is a woman; and show her honor as a fellow heir of the grace of life, so that your prayers will not be hindered.

Ephesians 5:25
Husbands, love our wives, just as Christ also loved the church and gave Himself up for her,

Ephesians 5:33
Nevertheless, each individual among you also is to love his own wife even as himself, and the wife must *see to it* that she respects her husband.

Hebrews 13:4
Marriage *is to be held* in honor among all, and the *marriage* bed *is to be* undefiled; for fornicators and adulterers God will judge.

1 Corinthians 7:4-7
The wife does not have authority over her own body, but the husband *does*; and likewise also the husband does not have authority over his own body, but the wife *does*. Stop depriving one another, except by agreement for a time, so that you may devote yourselves to prayer, and come together again so that Satan will not tempt you because of your lack of self-control. But this I say by way of concession, not of command. Yet I wish that all men were even as I myself am. However, each man has his own gift from God, own in this manner, and another in that.

Ecclesiastes 9:9
Enjoy life with the woman whom you love all the days of your fleeting life which He has given to you under the sun; for this is your reward in life and in you toil in which you have labored under the sun.

MIRACLES

Psalm 77:14
You are the God who works wonders; You have made known Your strength among the peoples.

MONEY

Ecclesiastes 5:10
He who loves money will not be satisfies with money, nor he who loves abundance *with its* income. This too is vanity.

1 Timothy 6:10
For the love of money is a root of all sorts of evil, and some by longing for it have wandered away from the faith and pierced themselves with many griefs.

Psalm 37:16
Better is the little of the righteous Than the abundance of many wicked.

Luke 16:10,11
"He who is faithful in a very little thing is faithful also in much; and he who is unrighteous in a very little thing is unrighteous also in much. Therefore is you have not been faithful in the *use of* unrighteous wealth, who will entrust the true *riches* to you?"

Philippians 4:19
And my God will supply all your needs according to His riches in glory in Christ Jesus.

OBEDIENCE

Deuteronomy 11:26-28
"See, I am setting before you today a blessing and a curse: the blessing, if you listen to the commandments of the Lord you God, which I am commanding you today; and the curse, if you do not listen to the commandments of the Lord your God, but turn aside from the way which I am commanding you today, by following other gods which you have not known."

Deuteronomy 27:10
"You shall write on the stones all the words of this law very distinctly."

John 14:15,23
"If you love Me, you will keep My commandments." Jesus answered and said to him, "If anyone loves Me, he will keep My word; and My Father will love him, and We will come to him and make Our abode with him."

1 John 5:3
For this is the love of God, that we keep His commandments; and His commandments are not burdensome.

PARENTS

Leviticus 19:3
'Every one of you shall reverence his mother and his father, and you shall keep My Sabbaths; I am the Lord your God.'

Ephesians 6:1-3
Children, obey your parents in the Lord, for this is right. Honor your father and mother (which is the first commandment with a promise), so that it may be well with you, and that you may live long on the earth.

PATIENCE

Psalm 37:7

Rest in the Lord and wait patiently for Him; Do not fret because of him who prospers in his way, Because of the man who carries out wicked schemes.

Hebrews 10:36

For you have need of endurance, so that when you have done the will of God, you may receive what was promised.

PEACE

John 14:27

"Peace I leave with you; My peace I give to you; not as the world gives do I give to you. Do not let your heart be troubled, nor let it be fearful."

Romans 5:1

Therefore, having been justified by faith, we have peace with God through our Lord Jesus Christ,

Colossians 1:20

and through Him to reconcile all things to Himself, having made peace through the blood of His cross; through Him, *I say*, whether things on earth or things in heaven.

Philippians 4:7

And the peace of God, which surpasses all comprehension, will guard your hearts and your minds in Christ Jesus.

John 16:33

"These things I have spoken to you, so that in Me you may have peace. In the world you have tribulation, but take courage; I have overcome the world."

PERSECUTION

Matthew 5:10-12
"Blessed are those who have been persecuted for the sake of righteousness, for theirs is the kingdom of heaven. Blessed are you when *people* insult you and persecute you, and falsely say all kinds of evil against you because of Me. Rejoice and be glad, for your reward in heaven is great; for in the same way they persecuted the prophets who were before you."

John 15:20
"Remember the word that I said to you, 'A slave is not greater than his master.' If they persecuted Me, they will also persecute you; if they kept My word, they will keep yours also."

Romans 12:14
Bless those who persecute you; bless and do not curse.

2 Timothy 3:12
Indeed, all who desire to live godly in Christ Jesus will be persecuted.

PRAYER

Psalm 34:15,17,18
The face of the Lord is against evildoers, To cut off the memory of them from the earth. *The righteous* cry, and the Lord hears And delivers them out of all their troubles. The Lord is near to the brokenhearted And saves those who are crushed in spirit.

Matthew 6:9-13
"Pray, then, in this way: 'Our Father who is in heaven, Hallowed be Your name. Your kingdom come. Your will be done, On earth as it is in heaven. Give us this day our daily bread. And forgive us our debts, as we also have forgiven our debtors. And do not lead us into temptation, but deliver us from evil. For Yours is the kingdom and the power and the glory forever. Amen."

Matthew 21:22
"And all things you ask in prayer, believing, you will receive."

Matthew 7:7,8
"Ask, and it will be given to you; seek, and you will find; knock, and it will be opened to you. For everyone who asks receives, and he who seeks finds, and to him who knocks it will be opened."

John 15:7
"If you abide in Me, and My words abide in you, ask whatever you wish, and it will be done for you."

1 Thessalonians 5:17
Pray without ceasing;

Philippians 4:6
Be anxious for nothing, but in everything by prayer and supplication with thanksgiving let your requests be made known to God.

RESURRECTION

Psalm 30:3, 41:10
O Lord, You have brought up my soul from Sheol; You have kept me alive, that I would not go down to the pit. But You, O Lord, be gracious to me and raise me up, That I may repay them.

1 Corinthians 15:3-8
For I delivered to you as of first importance what I also received, that Christ died for our sins according to the Scriptures, and that he was buried, and that He was raised on the third day according to the Scriptures. And that He appeared to Cephas, then to the twelve. After that He appeared to more than five hundred brethren at one time, most of whom remain until now, but some have fallen asleep; then he appeared to James, then to all the apostles; and last of all, as to one untimely born, He appeared to me also.

John 14:19
"After a little while the world will no longer see Me, but you *will* see Me; because I live, you will live also."

REVENGE

Romans 12:19
Never take you own revenge, beloved, but leave room for the wrath *of God*, for it is written, "Vengeance is mine, I will repay" says the Lord.

Matthew 5:38-41
"You have heard that it was said, 'An eye for an eye, and a tooth for a tooth.' But I say to you, do not resist an evil person; but whoever slaps you on your right cheek, turn the other to him also. If anyone wants to sue you and take your shirt, let him have your coat also. Whoever forces you to go one mile, go with him two."

Matthew 6:14
"For if you forgive others for their transgressions, your heavenly Father will also forgive you."

SALVATION

Exodus 15:2
"The Lord is my strength and song, and He has become my salvation; This is my God, and I will praise Him; My father's God, and I will extol Him."

Isaiah 55:6
Seek the Lord while He may be found; Call upon Him while He is near.

2 Corinthians 5:17
Therefore if anyone is in Christ, *he is* a new creature; the old things passed away; behold, new things have come.

SATAN

Ephesians 6:11
Put on the full armor of God, so that you will be able to stand firm against the schemes of the devil.

SEXUAL IMMORALITY

1 Thessalonians 4:3,4,7
For this is the will of God, your sanctification; *that is,* that you abstain from sexual immorality; that each of you know how to possess his own vessel in sanctification an honor, For God has not called us for the purpose of impurity, but in sanctification.

Hebrews 13:4
Marriage *is to be held* in honor among all, and the *marriage* bed *is to be* undefiled; for fornicators and adulterers God will judge.

2 Peter 2:9
then the Lord knows how to rescue the godly from temptation, and to keep the unrighteous under punishment for the day of judgment,

1 Corinthians 10:13
No temptation has overtaken you but such as is common to man; and God is faithful, who will not allow you to be tempted beyond what you are able, but with the temptation will provide the way of escape also, so that you will be able to endure it.

SHAME

Romans 9:33
just as it is written, "Behold, I lay in Zion a stone of stumbling and a rock of offense. And he who believes in Him will not be disappointed."

Isaiah 54:4,5
"Fear not, for you will not be put to shame; And do not feel humiliated, for you will not be disgraced; But you will forget the shame of your youth, And the reproach of your widowhood

you will remember no more. For your husband is your Maker, Whose name is the Lord of hosts; And your Redeemer is the Holy One of Israel, Who is called the God of all the earth."

Romans 10:11
For the Scripture says, "Whoever believes in Him will not be disappointed."

THANKFULNESS

1 Thessalonians 5:18
In everything give thanks; for this is God's will for you in Christ Jesus.

Psalm 95:2
Let us come before His presence with thanksgiving, Let us shout joyfully to Him with psalms.

Psalm 100:4
Enter His gates with thanksgiving *And* His courts with praise. Give thanks to Him, bless His name.

THOUGHTS

Matthew 15:18,19
"But the things that proceed out of the mouth come from the heart, and those defile the man. For out of the heart come evil thoughts, murders, adulteries, fornications, thefts, false witness, slanders."

Colossians 3:2
Set your mind on the things above, not on the things that are on the earth.

Romans 12:2
And do not be conformed to this world, but be transformed by the renewing of your mind, so that you may prove what the will of God is, that which is good and acceptable and perfect.

Philippians 2:5
Have this attitude in yourselves which was also in Christ Jesus.

TROUBLE

Psalm 9:9
The Lord also will be a stronghold for the oppressed, A stronghold in times of trouble;

Psalm 27:5
For in the day of trouble He will conceal me in His tabernacle; In the secret place of His tent He will hide me; He will lift me up on a rock.

Psalm 31:7,9
I will rejoice and be glad in Your lovingkindness, Because You have seen my affliction; You have known the troubles of my soul,

Psalm 55:22
"Cast your burden upon the Lord and He will sustain you; He will never allow the righteous to be shaken."

Psalm 46:1
God is our refuge and strength, A very present help in trouble.

Psalm 18:2,3
The Lord is my rock and my fortress and my deliverer, My God, my rock, in whom I take refuge; My shield and the horn of my salvation, my stronghold. I call upon the Lord, who is worthy to be praised, And I am saved from my enemies.

TRUST

Proverbs 3:5,6
Trust in the Lord with all your heart And do not lean on your own understanding. In all your ways acknowledge Him, And He will make your paths straight.

Job 13:15
"Though He slay me, I will hope in Him. Nevertheless I will argue my ways before Him."

Romans 8:37
But in all these things we overwhelmingly conquer through Him who loved us.

Psalm 37:3-5
Trust in the Lord and do good; Dwell in the land and cultivate faithfulness. Delight yourself in the Lord; And he will give you the desires of your heart. Commit your way to the Lord, Trust also in Him, and he will do it.

WISDOM

Proverbs 1:7
The fear of the Lord is the beginning of knowledge; Fools despise wisdom and instruction.

Psalm 1:1,2
How blessed is the man who does not walk in the counsel of the wicked, Nor stand in the path of sinners, Nor sit in the seat of scoffers! But his delight is in the law of the Lord, And in His law he meditates day and night.

Proverbs 3:13
How blessed is the man who finds wisdom And the man who gains understanding.

Colossians 3:16
Let the word of Christ richly well within you, with all wisdom teaching and admonishing one another with psalms *and* hymns *and* spiritual songs, singing with thankfulness in your hearts to God.

WORSHIP

Exodus 34:14
-for you shall not worship any other god, for the Lord, whose name is Jealous, is a jealous God-

Psalm 29:2
Ascribe to the Lord the glory due to His name; Worship the Lord in holy array.

Psalm 95:6
Come, let us worship and bow down, Let us kneel before the Lord our Maker.

ENDNOTES

1. Sadly, for author and family, Karen passed away on January 24, 2000. In spite of our loss, the truths presented here, illustrated in our marriage and life together, remain.

2. For more on marriage, see *Marriage and Family Life: A Christian Perspective* by Dr. Stan DeKoven.

3. For more on a theological view of depression, see Dr. Ken Chant's fascinating book *Dazzling Secrets for Despondent Saints*, available from Vision Publishing.

4. For more on career decisions, see *Assessment of Human Needs* by Dr. Stan DeKoven.

5. See *Substance Abuse Therapy* by Dr. Stan DeKoven.

6. Roberts, Allen, R. *Crisis Manangement and Brief Treatment*. Nelson-Hall Publisher. Chicago, 1998.

For Further Reference

1. Berman, Alan L. *Adolescent Suicide: Assessment and Intervention.* American Psychological Association, 1996.

2. Brown, S. L. *Counseling Victims of Violence.* Alexandria, VA: American Association for Counseling and Development, 1991.

3. Crabb, Lawrence. *Effective Biblical Counseling.* Grand Rapids, MI: Zondervan, 1977.

4. Johnson, K. *Trauma in the Lives of Children. Crisis and Stress Management Techniques for Teachers, Counselors, and Student Service Professionals.* Alameda, CA: Hunter House, 1989.

5. McWilliam, P. J., and Bailey, D. B., eds. *Working Together with Children and Families: Case Studies in Early Intervention.* Baltimore: Paul H. Brookes Publishing Co., 1991.

6. Nordgren, J. Chris, and Englund, Nicole. *Children and Disaster: A School Counselor's Handbook on How to Help.* University of South Dakota Disaster Mental Health Institute.

7. Pitcher, G.D., and Poland, S. *Crisis Intervention in the Schools.* New York: Guilford Press, 1992.

8. Roberts, A.R. (Ed.). *Crisis Intervention and Time-limited Congitive Therapy.* Thousand Oaks, CA: Sage, 1995.

9. Roberts, A.R. (Ed.). *Crisis Intervention Handbook: Assessment, Treatment, and Research.* Belmont, CA: Wadsworth, 1990.

10. Robinson, Edward H, Rotter, Joseph C., Fey, Mary Ann, and Vogel, Kenneth R. *Helping Children Cope with Fears and Stress.* Greensboro, NC, 1992.

11. Small, L. *The Brief Psychotherapies*. 2nd Ed. New York: Brunner/ Mazel, 1979.

12. Spirito, Anthony, and Overholser, James. *Evaluating and Treating Adolescent Suicide Attempters: From Research to Practice (Practical Resources for the Mental Health Professional)*. Academic Press, 2002.

13. Stone, Howard W. *Crisis Counseling*. Fortress Press, 1993.

14. Webb, Nancy Boyd. *Play Therapy with Children in Crisis: Individual, Group, and Family Treatment*. New York: Guilford Press, 1999.

The Teaching Ministry of Dr. Stan DeKoven

Dr. Stan DeKoven conducts seminars and professional workshops, both nationally and internationally, based on his books and extensive experience in Practical Christian Living. He is available for limited engagements at Church Seminars, retreats and conferences. For a complete listing of topics books, we invite you to contact:

Dr. Stan DeKoven, President
Vision International College & University
Walk in Wisdom Seminars
1520 Main Street, Suite C
Ramona, CA 92065
760-789-4700 (in California) or
1-800-9 VISION
www.vision.edu

Other helpful books by Dr. DeKoven on related topics include:

Journey to Wholeness: Restoration of the Soul
Marriage and Family Life: A Christian Perspective
Grief Relief: Prescriptions for Pain After Significant Loss
On Belay! Introduction to Christian Counseling
Family Violence: Patterns of Destruction
Forty Days to the Promise: A Way Through the Wilderness
Parenting on Purpose
12 Steps to Wholeness
Human Devleopment (with Bohac)
Group Dynamics (with Bohac)

Printed in the United States
24805LVS00007B/70-75